# THE BEST RECIPES FOR
# BABIES & TODDLERS

RENÉE ELLIOTT

# THE BEST RECIPES FOR BABIES & TODDLERS

**More than 100 easy recipes for delicious purées and meals**

DUNCAN BAIRD PUBLISHERS

LONDON

I dedicate this book to the family I was born into and the family I gave birth to.

**THE BEST RECIPES FOR BABIES & TODDLERS**
Renée Elliott

First published in the United Kingdom and Ireland in 2010 by
Duncan Baird Publishers Ltd
Sixth Floor, Castle House
75–76 Wells Street
London W1T 3QH

Conceived, created and designed by Duncan Baird Publishers

**Managing Editor:** Grace Cheetham
**Editor:** Nicole Bator
**Managing Designer:** Manisha Patel
**Designer:** Luana Gobbo
**Commissioned photography:** Simon Smith
**Food Stylist:** Mari Mererid Williams
**Prop Stylist:** Wei Tang

British Library Cataloguing-in-Publication Data:
A CIP record for this book is available from the British Library

ISBN: 978-1-84483-874-5

10 9 8 7 6 5 4 3 2

Typeset in Frutiger, Univers, Clarendon and Berranger Hand
Colour reproduction by Scanhouse
Printed in Thailand by Imago

**Publisher's note**
While every care has been taken in compiling the recipes for this book, Duncan Baird Publishers, or any other persons who have been involved in working on this publication, cannot accept responsibility for any errors or omissions, inadvertent or not, that may be found in the recipes or text, nor for any problems that may arise as a result of preparing one of these recipes. If you are pregnant or breastfeeding or have any special dietary requirements or medical conditions, it is advisable to consult a medical professional before following any of the recipes contained in this book.

**Notes on the recipes**
Unless otherwise stated:
Use organic ingredients
Use large eggs, and medium fruit and vegetables
Use fresh ingredients, including herbs
Do not mix metric and imperial measurements
1 tsp = 5ml   1 tbsp = 15ml   1 cup = 250ml

Symbols are used to identify even small amounts of an ingredient, such as the seeds symbol for sesame oil. Dairy foods in this book may include cow's, goat's or sheep's milk. The vegetarian symbol is given to recipes using cheese; please check the manufacturer's labelling before purchase to ensure cheeses are vegetarian. Ensure that only the relevantly identified foods are given to anyone with a food allergy or intolerance.

**Acknowledgments**
Huge thanks, hugs and kisses to my husband Brian and my kids for eating my food and being so patient; my mom for her recipes; Julia for her total support; Nathalie for caring for my children; Allison for helping out without being asked; Veronica for her encouragement; Molly for tuna pie and prawn bake; and Maggie for the knife. Thank you to Borra, Grace, Luana and Nicole. Without you there simply wouldn't be a book. And to Suzannah Olivier, whose book *What Should I Feed My Baby?* inspired me when I was a new mother.

# contents

## KEY TO SYMBOLS

 Vegetarian: Contains no meat, poultry, game, fish, shellfish or animal by-products.

 Wheat-free: Contains no wheat, wheat flour or wheat products.

 Gluten-free: Contains no gluten-based grains or products, including wheat, barley, rye, oat, spelt and Kamut.

 Dairy-free: Contains no dairy products, including milk, cheese, yogurt, kefir or butter.

 Egg-free: Contains no eggs or egg products.

 Nut-free: Contains no nuts (almonds, Brazil nuts, cashew nuts, chestnuts, coconut, hazelnuts, macadamia nuts, peanuts, pecans, pine nuts, pistachio nuts and walnuts) or nut oils.

 Seed-free: Contains no seeds (flax, hemp, pumpkin, safflower, sesame and sunflower) or seed oils.

# foreword

I am the jars of baby food my mom fed me as an infant. I am the endless pots of Creole stew she stirred on the stove. I am my mom chopping onions at the counter. My mom taking yet another batch of cookies out of the oven. My dad teaching us how to tie up the tomato plants and when to pick the ripe summer squash. My brother and sisters standing in the slanting autumn sun crunching cucumbers sprinkled with salt.

I am the university student who studied health and ageing. The adventurer who followed her heart and came to England. The employee who realized she had to love and believe in what she did. I am the entrepreneur who started Planet Organic. And I am the mother who learned to cook all over again. I am not, however, a trained chef. I, like you, simply have to feed my family.

Growing up, the kitchen table was where we sat together to share food; where I watched my mom roll out endless pastry to make endless pies; and where as a family we chatted over morning coffee. Food is important to me and, as I have grown up and had my own children, it has become even more important.

I was running Planet Organic when I had my daughter Jessica, and between caring for her and working, I had no time at all. Then I had Nicholas, continued working and then had Cassandra. With three children, putting meals together had to be easier than ever.

Like everyone else, I want convenience in my life. All too often, however, convenience comes at the expense of health, whether through eating processed foods or ready meals, or swallowing a pill to feel better when we are sick. Twenty years ago, I realized that there was a better way to eat, live and age. I started to question the majority of food that was for sale in the supermarkets. I learned about organic foods, nutrition and alternative therapies, such as homeopathy and acupuncture, and I decided that I wasn't willing to take convenience at the expense of my, or my children's, health.

But even I, who love food and cooking, don't want to be – and can't be – in the kitchen all day. So this book is about making things easy. It's about quick, uncomplicated food, like boiling some pasta or opening a tin of sardines, and it's also about slow-cooked, rich autumn stews and long-rise bread. Above all, it's about giving your baby the best, healthiest start in life and creating healthy habits that will last a lifetime.

It is, however, no ordinary cookbook. It combines my own knowledge with the knowledge I have gained from other experts, ideas that make sense to me and methods that worked with my kids. It will change the way you eat and think about food. You'll see many familiar ingredients here, alongside many that will probably be new to you. Don't worry. You'll soon understand exactly what kombu, kefir and miso are, and why I think these 'unusual' foods are so important for your child.

My approach may present for you a completely different way of eating and cooking – one that will create an entirely new relationship between you and your food. I'm not saying that this is the only way to wean and feed your baby. I'm saying, try this. I think it's the best way. But don't be too rigid; there aren't a lot of definite rights and wrongs. Many ideas and methods for babies have not yet been proven, and new research emerges all the time. So, I say, take advice – and then listen to your intuition.

Understanding the choices you have when feeding your child is so important, especially if you don't know a lot about food, your body or how to create good health through good nutrition. Eating healthily is vital, and eating organic is the best thing for you. Don't worry about what you cooked or ate in the past; try something new. Focus on today. Be happy you have this book in your hands now. Be grateful that you know more now or are willing to explore and learn.

I can't emphasize enough how important it is to make changes slowly so that it isn't stressful and so that you incorporate them into your life going forward. Introduce a few new good foods and get rid of a few old bad habits each month. If you do too much too quickly, you won't persevere. Take it slowly and make these changes to last a lifetime. If you have just become pregnant, you can start making changes to your family's diet now or any time over the months until your baby is born. If your newborn is ready to wean, you can start now. Anyone can do this.

I can't wait for you to find your own favourites in these pages. For you to try different whole grains, different flavours, different techniques. To think about adding extra nutrition when you can. To realize that every bite counts and to waste fewer of them than you are now – but to still make a treat of organic chocolate every now and then. To discover the recipes that your child will want you to cook again and again. To find the way to health and vitality.

Renée Elliott

# introduction

For most of us, having children delivers a massive jolt to our sense of priorities. I'm no exception. I had built my career and lifestyle around my love of food and interest in health, but it all took on an entirely new significance when I had my children and realized that I was completely responsible for their nutrition and well-being. Suddenly, what had been interesting became incredibly important. I knew that what I taught my children about food when they were young would be with them for a lifetime. Cooking delicious, homemade food became a huge priority for me, as well as an immense pleasure. If you want to give your child – and yourself – a healthier, more satisfying way of eating, this book is for you.

I know from my own experience that being a new mother, particularly a first-time mother, is hard. Your life has been turned on its head, you may not be sleeping much, you never seem to have enough time to do everything you have to do – and this adorable but demanding little person is with you all the time. I now have three young children and, though I like to think I'm doing the best feeding the third, I learned the most with the first because we had so much time together, and she was the only one seeking my attention.

With each new addition to our family, I adapted what I had learned. This book has evolved from that experience. It's about ease, variety and taste and, above all, about optimizing nutrition and health for your baby and yourself, not only now but for the rest of your lives. Whether you are just learning to cook with this book and this baby or you are trying to figure out how to introduce organic, wholesome, homemade food into your busy life, now is your opportunity to get started. It won't be long before you'll be off and running: swapping ingredients, adding a little of this and a little of that and changing recipes to meet your child's growing tastes and health needs.

## Why Is Health So Important?

Some people worry about giving their child a good education or getting him to excel at sports or a musical instrument, but for me the most important thing is health. You could have the brightest, most gifted, most well-educated child, but without good health, he won't go far. With good health, he can achieve his dreams and fulfil his potential. And it's easier to be happy when you're healthy.

I'm not just talking about your child being well today or when he's a teenager. This is about creating health and healthy habits to last a lifetime, without so many of the diseases that affect people in our society. Being well now is also about ageing well – for your child and for yourself, so you can enjoy him and his children for many years to come.

Unfortunately, you can eat bad food for years and feel okay – but you could be slowly creating unease in your body that becomes disease as you age. Heart disease, liver disease and diabetes, all of which have been linked to diet, take years to develop.

There's so much in our world that is damaging, and which we can control very little, or not at all. Polluted air, chemically treated water, formaldehyde-laced carpets and curtains, noxious cleaning materials used in the exaggerated war on germs and, of course, stress all take their toll on the body. While you can't do that much about those things, you can control what your family eats. What you put in your child's mouth are the only ingredients that his body has to grow and to nurture and repair itself.

**Good Food versus Bad Food**

Think about the ingredients you give your body every day. Don't assume that a food is good for you simply because it's allowed to be sold. The truth is that many farmers, manufacturers and retailers are not concerned about your health. They're running a business. Some sell good food; some sell bad. How can you tell the difference?

Highly processed, refined products like store-bought cakes, breads, doughnuts, sausages, fast food, fizzy drinks and sweets belong to the bad-food category. The length of the ingredients list is a strong clue as to whether a food is good or bad. If the list is long, particularly with words you don't understand, chances are it's a food you and your child would be better off without. My motto is: if you don't know what it is, don't put it into your body. If your granny wouldn't cook with it, forget it.

Basic ingredients to avoid are hydrogenated fats, monosodium glutamate (MSG), and artificial flavourings, colourings, additives and preservatives. Hydrogenated fats are laden with trans fats, which are highly processed fats that the human body cannot process. These fats tend to congregate at fatty sites in the body and are difficult to excrete. They're used because they are cheap, easy to work with and extend a food's shelf life. Artificial preservatives also make bad, cheap food last longer than it should, and artificial flavours, colours and additives make it taste and look better. A chocolate chip cookie made with hydrogenated fat and artificial ingredients can sit on the supermarket shelf for months, losing what little nutritional value it has as it ages. The same cookie made with butter and natural ingredients will go out of date more quickly because its ingredients are perishable. You can choose to eat the fresh cookie or the old cookie. It's up to you. But who wants to eat old food? I don't.

Good food comes directly from nature: fruit, vegetables, grains, nuts, seeds, dairy, fish and meat. It does not contain chemicals or lots of additives. Good food is organic food. Some processed foods, including biscuits and snacks, can be good, but when you read the label, you should understand the ingredients list – and the shorter the list, the better.

## Buy Organic

With all food, buy organic wherever possible. Conventional, chemical-based farming, which developed after World War II, is all about quantity – growing as much food as possible. Farmers and crops that use nitrogen fertilizer become dependent on pesticides, herbicides and fungicides. Conventional farming routinely uses hundreds of these chemicals. Designed to kill bugs, weeds and plant diseases, these poisons stay on our food, are eaten by birds, go into our water, are carried by the air and are pretty much everywhere on the planet now, from the Arctic to the tropics. If you want to avoid eating these chemicals, choose organic.

Government guidelines set 'safe' levels for the amount of poisonous residue that can linger on our food and be ingested on a daily basis. These levels, however, are set for individual foods and are based on what is considered 'safe' for a normal, healthy adult – not for a baby or toddler, or an old person, or someone with a compromised immune system. This means that there is an acceptable amount of poison that can be on the apple you give to your toddler, but the government guidelines don't take into account the fact that he is little – and they don't consider the cocktail of chemicals he eats over the course of each day by combining different foods.

Organic food, on the other hand, is about quality. It's about growing healthy soil, healthy plants and healthy animals to create healthy people. Organic doesn't depend on chemical fertilizers or poisons to grow food or resolve problems in farming. It doesn't wage war on nature – a war, I think, we'll never win. Emerging research funded by the European Union also shows that organic food contains higher levels of some nutrients, including vitamin C; essential minerals, such as calcium, magnesium and iron; cancer-fighting antioxidants; and omega-3 fats. If you want the best-quality food, buy organic. It's that simple. If you're unable to buy all organic, then choose organic for the things your family eats the most of and buy organic meat, eggs and dairy products.

## Genetically Modified Foods

A genetically modified (GM) food is any ingredient whose DNA has been artificially altered in a laboratory to achieve a desired characteristic. Some crops are modified to make them resistant to drought or to frost. Others have been developed to produce built-in pesticides to ward off pests and diseases, and they cannot be washed off before the food is eaten.

GM foods are often given genes from completely different food sources. This raises the question of whether a GM soya bean engineered with nut proteins in order to boost the bean's omega-3 fats could pose a danger to someone with a nut allergy. And it's not just the harm to humans that has many worried about GM. Little can be done to prevent a field planted with GM crops from contaminating neighbouring non-GM crops; and almost no testing has been done to determine the effects of genetic modification on other species in the ecosystem.

GM foods were introduced into the food chain in the 1990s, so it's still too soon to know what the lasting effects of these foods will be on our health, environment and economies. There's no reason you and your child should eat them and be part of a massive experiment on public health. GM foods are labelled in some countries. Find out if they are in yours and then avoid them. If GM foods are not labelled where you live, then that's another reason to buy organic, which excludes GM completely.

## Cooking from Scratch

Now that you understand why good, natural, organic food is so important, it's time to get started. If you're worried that cooking from scratch will be too hard or too much work, stop worrying. The recipes in this book are easy, provide your baby with the best possible nutrition and taste a lot better than jarred baby foods.

BATCH COOKING: If you can, cook up a big batch of different dishes, freeze them in ice-cube trays and then transfer them to airtight, freezerproof containers for later use. Little cubes of food defrost quickly (see page 18), and having a variety of different foods to hand will make feeding your baby much easier.

BALANCED MEALS: Serving good, balanced meals really is easy, and the pages that follow will cover all the basics. In general, you want to make sure to serve protein, vegetables, fruit, complex carbohydrate, good oils and filtered water every day. Protein, made of amino acids, provides the building blocks for our bodies and forms the basis of our cells. Growing children need more protein than adults. Complex carbohydrates, such as whole grains, wholemeal breads and unpeeled white and sweet potatoes, provide steady energy. Avoid simple carbohydrates, such as white flour and white rice, and sugar, because they all wreak havoc on blood sugar levels.

## Ingredients & Equipment

Whether it's food or utensils made of certain materials, I try to make sure that everything I cook with is safe for my children. Here are some of my essentials:

**WHOLE GRAINS:** One of the most important items in my storecupboard, whole grains add richness and variety to your diet. They can help lower the risk of type 2 diabetes and have been shown to protect against childhood asthma. Most people eat wheat and corn regularly, and perhaps some rye, but it's important to rotate these with other whole grains, such as brown rice, barley, quinoa, spelt, Kamut, millet, amaranth and buckwheat. You can bake with these grains, make stews, pancakes, breads, desserts – the list is endless. I strongly suggest buying only organic whole grains. Non-organic grains carry pesticide residues and higher levels of naturally occurring mycotoxins, which may cause illness.

Unfortunately, many people go days or longer without eating any whole grains. A grain is whole when it still contains the bran, germ and endosperm. The bran and germ of the grain are rich in fibre, vitamins, minerals, antioxidants and healthy fats. The endosperm is high in simple carbohydrates and low in nutrients. When grain is refined, the bran and germ are removed, leaving just the endosperm – so that's what you get in white bread and white pasta. The body quickly breaks down the endosperm's simple sugars and releases them into the bloodstream. This is one reason why eating refined grains and refined grain products, such as white flour, white bread, white rice and white pasta, has such a harsh effect on blood sugar levels and energy. These products have been so processed that all the natural goodness, including the fibre, has been taken out. If you look at their labels, you'll see that thiamine, niacin and B vitamins have been added back in – but these are synthetic vitamins, not natural ones, and we don't know how good they are. Natural is always better, and with whole grains, you know that all the goodness is still inside.

It's fine to have some white pasta or a crusty baguette every now and again. But if you have white toast for breakfast, a white-bread sandwich for lunch, white-flour biscuits in the afternoon and white pasta for supper, day after day and week after week, then you're getting too little nutrition – and too much wheat.

Wheat has been so hybridized over the years that it bears little resemblance to the grain first domesticated 10,000 years ago. Hybridization, especially the intensive form practised by modern industrial agriculture, has changed the structure and gluten level in the wheat. This, along with over-consumption, may be why so many people today have wheat sensitivities. Eating a wide variety of foods is the best way to get a broad range of nutrients, so make it a point to diversify. Buy wholemeal rye bread, brown rice crackers and spelt or corn pasta, for example, and experiment with different flours for your baking.

**WHOLEMEAL FLOUR:** When I bake, I use wholemeal spelt flour. Spelt, a relative of wheat, is an ancient grain that, unlike wheat, has not been hybridized and manipulated over the years in order to make it easier to harvest and use. Spelt remains as nature originally created it. For breads and cookies, I use 100 per cent wholemeal spelt flour; for cakes or cupcakes, I use a 50/50 mixture of wholemeal and white spelt flours for a lighter texture. Using wholemeal flour makes treats and snacks nutritious. You can easily change your existing recipes to use wholemeal, preferably spelt, flour. For cookies or other things that don't really rise, do a straight substitution. For cakes and breads, substitute half of the white flour with wholemeal flour.

**HEALTHY FATS:** Good-quality fats are essential, especially for children. This may sound counter-intuitive considering how much our society focuses on low-fat foods. It's important to realize, however, that not all fat is bad, and people generally aren't fat from eating too much fat. Blaming obesity on fat is too simplistic. People are fat from eating badly, eating too much of the wrong foods and not getting enough exercise.

Kids need a certain amount of fat in their diets. Good fats are monounsaturated and polyunsaturated fats, which include essential fatty acids. Essential fats reduce the risk of cancer, heart disease, allergies, arthritis, eczema, depression, fatigue, infections and more. Some of the good fats I feed my kids include olive oil, flaxseed oil, hemp seed oil, oily fish oils, almonds and pumpkin seeds. Yogurt, which isn't very high in fat, is another great choice, so buy full-fat natural yogurt for your baby. I like to cook with butter because it's a good high-heat, natural fat, but I don't use it every day and I don't use a lot. Avoid hydrogenated fats, including margarines that are made of hydrogenated or partially hydrogenated fats. If you want to use margarines, choose organic ones, which are made with non-hydrogenated oils.

**COW'S MILK ALTERNATIVES:** Our bodies are designed to consume our mother's milk and then move on to solid foods. So, when a baby weans, he should get his nutrition from food, not from cow's milk. No other animal continues to drink milk after it has weaned. Because we don't need milk after weaning, we begin to lose the ability to produce our own enzymes to digest it; as we get older, milk becomes more difficult to digest. Furthermore, cow's milk is pasteurized, which means that all the enzymes in it that help us to digest it have been killed.

Milk is not as great a source of calcium as many people believe, either. For calcium to be well used by the body, it must be consumed with the right balance of magnesium, and milk contains very little magnesium. Foods with a perfect calcium/magnesium balance include nuts and seeds, and vegetables such as spinach and broccoli, so make sure your child gets lots of these foods.

If you do choose to give your child cow's milk, buy organic milk: it contains no antibiotic or hormone residues, and research has shown that it has higher levels of vitamin E, other antioxidants and omega-3 essential fatty acids.

Although I avoid giving my children cow's milk, other milk products can be nutritious. Cultured milk products, such as yogurt and cheese, are fermented, making them healthier and easier to digest. Yogurt is great because it contains live bifidus and acidophilus cultures, which are the good bacteria that should inhabit the gut. They keep harmful bacteria under control, ensure that the body produces vitamins and enzymes and keep down the level of toxins in the body, preventing potential diseases. Kefir contains those live cultures, plus healthy yeast cultures, which help restore a better balance to the gut flora, so it's even better. Wherever feasible, opt for products made from goat's and sheep's milk, which have smaller fat globules and are more easily digested than cow's milk.

Once a baby has weaned, he can drink water. Milk substitutes, such as oat milk, rice milk or soya milk, are good for breakfast cereals, but use soya milk and rice milk in moderation. Soya contains isoflavones, or hormone (oestrogen) mimics, which can disrupt a baby's normal hormone balance. In countries where soya and its products are consumed traditionally, they're usually fermented and eaten in small quantities – not as a substitute for animal protein. Rice milk contains low levels of arsenic, so children from one to five years should not have too much of it. If a child drinks a lot of soya or rice milk, he'll drink a lot in proportion to his body weight; as a result, he'll be exposed to more of these compounds. Give your child water to drink and let him get calcium from food.

**NATURAL SUGARS:** Originally used only in sweet foods, sugar is now added to many savoury foods as well. Concentrated, simple sugar hits the bloodstream quickly and causes a rapid increase in blood sugar levels. This gives you an energy surge that is followed by a quick drop as the body rushes to rebalance. This stress, repeated over and over, is not good. Diabetes is the extreme form of blood sugar imbalance and has become more and more common in children and young people. Eating too much sugar and too many refined grains exacerbates the problem and increases a child's risk of developing diabetes. Furthermore, sugar that is not used by the body is converted into fat.

It's easy to give in to your child's sugar cravings, but you may create a lifetime addiction to it if you do. Your baby is so malleable, and you mould his tastes, so start him off on a different route. He doesn't know about strawberry-flavoured sweetened yogurt, so serve natural. Refrain from sweetening sour fruits, such as raspberries or red currants, and let him experience their natural flavour. Some children actually like tart or sour foods, and others will develop a taste for them over time. If your child says 'yuck' to something once, try again another time because his taste will change and develop. I can't believe that I didn't like Brussels sprouts when I was a kid – I love them now.

White and brown sugar, glucose, molasses, honey and maple syrup are all simple sugars. Fruit contains fructose, a simple sugar, but the body must first convert fructose into glucose, which means that it releases slowly. So even though fruits contain simple sugars, they are, in general, much better than sweets and other sugars.

A special word about honey: do not give honey to babies younger than one year because it carries a slight risk of botulism.

The best sweetener is brown rice malt, which is made up mostly of complex sugars and, therefore, releases more slowly into the bloodstream. To convert the sugar in your recipes to brown rice malt, use 185ml/6fl oz/¾ cup brown rice malt for every 220g/7¾oz/1 cup sugar, and reduce liquids by 60ml/2fl oz/¼ cup.

You'll notice that there aren't a lot of desserts in this book. That's because there's really no point in serving them, especially every day. A sugar habit is a terrible thing to create in your child. Fill him up instead with good food, not sweets that contain empty calories and no nutritional value. Serve sweets occasionally, yes, as a special treat. But daily? No. And wait as long as possible to give your child sugar. You can certainly wait until his first birthday and then let the birthday cake be his first taste of sugar. (There's a great cake recipe for you on page 159.)

Help control your child's sugar cravings by reducing the regularity of sweets. I don't give dessert after every meal because it sets up an expectation for something sweet and means some kids will fight with you by not eating their food and waiting for dessert. Take the dessert away and that problem disappears.

Finally, beware of 'sugar-free' foods. More often than not, this means artificial sweeteners, such as saccharine, aspartame and sorbitol – all of which have been linked to health problems. As much as I dislike sugar and do everything I can to limit it in my children's diets, it is better than artificial sweeteners, which no one should consume.

**REDUCED SALT:** All foods naturally contain sodium, which our bodies need. Eating too much added salt, however, is linked to all sorts of diseases, and children's kidneys struggle if made to deal with added salt. Your child's palate is pure; help shape it by making food without added salt. Wait until after one year to introduce salt and then use it only very sparingly. If you eat out a lot, eat processed foods or are in the habit of adding salt without really thinking about it, your own palate will need time to readjust and realize, for example, that a bowl of steamed broccoli drizzled with olive oil doesn't need salt. Vegetables don't need it, and anything with cheese doesn't usually need it. To satisfy a salt craving in an older child, offer toasted seaweed, like nori, as a snack.

**NON-TOXIC STORAGE CONTAINERS:** I store and serve food in little metal containers with plastic lids that don't come into contact with the food. Other good alternatives to plastic are glass or ceramic. Plastic contains harmful chemicals, including phthalates (the softer the plastic, the higher the phthalate content). Studies by Greenpeace show that some of these chemicals may interfere with the hormone systems that regulate normal growth and reproductive development in children. Kids can also ingest hazardous chemicals from plastic toys. Plastics are difficult to recycle, too. They either sit in landfills or are burned, often emitting dioxins and heavy metals. If you do use plastic, always let the food you're storing cool completely before you put it in a plastic container to reduce the risk of anything harmful leaching into the food.

STAINLESS STEEL COOKWARE: Good stainless steel cookware is ideal for everyday use. It can be heated to a high temperature, you can use any utensils with it and it lasts a long time. A well-seasoned cast iron pan is great, too.

Non-stick cookware has its conveniences, but just like plastic, it contains harmful toxins that can seep into your child's food. Perfluorooctanoic acid, or PFOA, also known as C8, is a chemical used to bond the non-stick coating to the pan. In early 2006, the United States Environmental Protection Agency (EPA) labelled PFOA a likely carcinogen and asked eight American companies to work toward its elimination by 2015. This is why I would never use non-stick cookware on a regular basis – it's just not worth the risk. If you do use it occasionally – and, I admit, it's great for making pancakes – make sure you don't heat it too high, never use metal utensils, which can scrape through the coating, and always open a window or turn on an extractor fan to remove potentially toxic fumes from your kitchen.

Avoid aluminium, too. Although more research needs to be done, cooking with aluminium pans has been linked to Alzheimer's disease; deodorants containing aluminium have been linked to breast cancer; and aluminium has been linked to several skeletal and neurological disorders. Until this is proven or not proven, I think it's best avoided.

OTHER EQUIPMENT: A good blender or small food processor is essential. You'll use it for everything from puréeing baby food to making things like smoothies and breadcrumbs. Get yourself a good all-round vegetable knife and an inexpensive vegetable scrubber. You shouldn't peel vegetables because much of the fibre is in the skin and a lot of nutrition is just under it, so you need to scrub them.

## Cooking Techniques
The recipes in this book focus heavily on nutrient-rich whole foods. Here are a few basic techniques that will help you master the art of cooking with whole foods.

SOAKING WHOLE GRAINS: In both traditional and modern cultures where whole grains are widely used, cooks take care to properly prepare them in order to maximize their nutrients and ease digestion. This means soaking the grain in warm, acidified water prior to cooking. It doesn't really take more time; you just have to think ahead.

All grains contain phytic acid in their outer layer, which can combine with minerals in the intestinal tract and block absorption, leading, in time, to mineral deficiencies. Soaking grains for at least seven hours or, even better, overnight, stimulates the grain's enzymes, which break down and neutralize the phytic acid. Once neutralized, phytic acid can be an important anti-cancer nutrient. Soaking also partially breaks down the proteins in grains, particularly gluten, to make them easier to digest. To soak whole grains, put the amount of grain you plan to cook in a saucepan and cover with the amount of warm water stated in the recipe. Stir in one tablespoon of kefir or yogurt and leave it to soak for seven hours or overnight, then cook without draining. If there is any history of dairy allergies in your family, rinse the grains before cooking.

**DRIED BEANS:** I always cook my own beans, and I never get bloated from them. The trick is to soak them overnight in double the amount of warm water and two tablespoons of lemon juice or vinegar. This rehydrates the beans and neutralizes the phytic acid and enzyme inhibitors. The next day, rinse the beans well, add fresh water for cooking, bring to the boil and boil for ten minutes, skimming any scum, which contains the difficult-to-digest complex sugars. Then add kombu, a seaweed, that helps soften the beans, makes them easier to digest and adds nutrients and flavour.

**STEAMING:** If you're not going to eat vegetables raw, steaming is the best way to cook them. Steaming retains nutrients that are lost in other types of cooking. When you boil vegetables, it is very easy to overcook them and lose valuable minerals. Until babies are able to chew their food, vegetables should be steamed until completely soft; afterwards, they should always be slightly crunchy.

## Time to Feed Your Baby

I approach weaning and feeding my children differently from a lot of the methods out there. The truth is, no one really knows the best way to do a lot of things we have to do in life, but my method makes sense to me and has worked with my own kids.

Your baby's immune and digestive systems are still developing and are very delicate in the first two years, so start slowly. I like to start with one food at a time. This makes it easier to identify the source of any reaction your baby might have, which is harder to do if he eats four or five different foods in one day and then develops a splotchy face. If you're serving one food at time and your baby has a reaction, you can simply stop serving that food and try again after eight weeks to see if he can handle it.

**WHEN TO INTRODUCE FOODS:** Raw fruit is an excellent way to start weaning because it's gentle on the baby's system, easy to digest and very nutritious. In addition to fruit, I recommend giving him vegetables, whole grains, pulses and good fats from four to six months. I like to give the baby's system time to get used to solid foods, so I wait until a couple of months later to introduce fish and meats. I don't introduce grains such as wheat, rye and spelt until one year because they contain gluten. Gluten is one of the most common proteins to which people are intolerant, so it makes sense to wait until the baby's system is more developed. Anyway, it's not like you have to give him gluten; as you will see, there is a huge range of gluten-free foods you can choose from. Eggs, cheese, nuts and certain fruits and vegetables are introduced between 12 and 24 months. See the charts in each chapter to determine if a food is appropriate at a specific age.

If you're introducing foods in the sequence I recommend and you do sometimes have to use jarred food, be aware that many contain ingredients such as milk or gluten that you won't want to introduce to your baby until a certain age. Always read the labels and buy organic. Opt for plain fruit and thicken it with instant millet or brown rice flakes.

**EATING ENOUGH:** Babies have a strong survival instinct and will usually eat unless they're full or something is wrong, so feed your baby until he won't eat any more. Let him have a small toy at meals when he's little and he'll be happier to sit still and eat. Take the toys away when he begins feeding himself – his hands will be busy. For babies and toddlers who may not eat much at meal times, offer snacks during the day to make sure they're getting enough food and variety. You can cut out the snacking when he's older.

Not all babies are chubby; many are long and slender, so don't compare yours to others. If you're worried that he isn't eating enough, weigh him each month and plot his weight on a growth chart. As long as he stays at the same percentile, he's fine. If he's not maintaining the same percentile, consult your doctor.

**STORING & REHEATING FOOD:** Each recipe includes storage instructions, so you can plan ahead. I suggest making batches of food in the first few months and freezing them in ice-cube trays. This will save you lots of time and provide you with a variety of foods that you can mix and match when you don't have the time or energy to cook fresh.

Little cubes of fruit, vegetables and grains defrost quickly, either in the fridge or heated in a pan over a medium heat, and some can be heated simply by putting the baby's bowl in a larger bowl of boiling water, which also keeps the food warm while you feed. Rice, however, should always be heated through until it is hot to kill any bacteria. Always thoroughly defrost meat, poultry and fish cubes in the fridge before reheating.

**FOOD SAFETY:** I try not to get too obsessive about germs and bacteria. I think that once babies are six months old, a reasonable exposure to everyday germs is a good thing because it helps to build a strong immune system. Living in a sterile environment does not. Just keep things clean, don't mix raw and cooked meats, and cook eggs and meats thoroughly for little children.

**ADDING NUTRITION:** We should feed ourselves the best we can all the time, but we don't, so add nutrition wherever you can. Here are some tricks to adding a little more oomph to each day. (These all must be age appropriate.)

• Always serve healthy fats (see page 13). Mix good oil into purées, pastas or steamed veggies. Sprinkle seeds or toasted nori over rice or salads. Add chopped bean sprouts to sandwiches. Use yogurt with breakfast cereals or mix it with cucumber for a snack.

• Focus on healthy snacks, such as crispbreads, unsweetened popcorn and low-salt tortilla chips. Organic nuts, seeds and spreads, such as tahini, are great, too. Avoid peanuts, though – they're a pesticide-laden crop. If you do serve them, buy organic.

• At meals, offer two vegetables of different colours, one cooked and one raw, to provide different nutrients. You can serve one before the main dish. Vegetable sticks with olive oil, mayonnaise, mustard or hummus for dipping are great. Use ketchup occasionally for variety, but it's sweet, so don't become too dependent on it.

• Even if your child has a great diet, it's worth considering a good-quality, food-state multi-mineral and vitamin to ensure he's getting everything he needs.

One of the biggest lessons to learn is to not get stressed. I can't say this enough to any mother – first time or third time – and I have to say it to myself all the time. Do the best you can. Have some great days, don't worry about the not-so-great ones and strive always to improve. Establish a routine with your child when you can. His system gets used to eating, napping and sleeping at certain times, and the steadier the routine, the easier life is. Give your child the best food you can. Try to make as many mouthfuls as you can count toward his health and well-being. He may rebel when he's older and eat rubbish for a while, but kids tend to go back to what they know – and what makes them feel good. Use this book to give your baby the best possible start in life, and to create health, vitality and happiness for a lifetime.

# weaning

It's hard to believe how much your baby has grown already. By four months, she may be showing signs that she's ready to start trying some solid foods. By six months, she'll definitely need to extend her culinary range beyond breast milk or formula. Her digestive system, however, is still developing, so it's important to start gently. That's why the puréed fruits, vegetables, whole grains and pulses in this chapter are so ideal for weaning. From sweet Banana Mash and Butternut Squash Purée to nutty Baby Brown Rice Purée and creamy Flageolet Purée, these first foods will give your baby the best nutritional start. She'll love experiencing the delicious, mild flavours of these new foods – and you'll love how easy they are to prepare. This is the beginning of your child's relationship with food, so give her the best you can, with lots of variety, and she'll be on her way to a lifetime of good eating.

*Avocado Mash (see page 28)*

# 4 to 6 months

Starting your baby on her first foods is an exciting time. She can begin solids at four months but can go for up to six months before she really needs nutrition from sources other than breast milk or formula, so don't rush to wean. The older she is, the more developed her digestive system and the better it will digest and assimilate solid foods. However, if she's grabbing your fork while you're eating, it's probably time to start, and not all babies can wait until six months. Teeth are another sign that she's ready for solids. If you offer her the first spoonful of food and it goes straight into her mouth and is swallowed, then she is definitely ready because a baby's reflex is for the tongue to push outward. This is the action for breastfeeding and also ensures she doesn't take things she shouldn't into her mouth. So if the first spoonful comes back out, she may not be ready. Even if it comes out, though, and you think that she is no longer satisfied by only breast milk or formula, you can try holding the spoon at her lips and see if she sucks the food in.

## How to Wean

Your baby's immune and digestive systems are still developing and are not ready for all foods at once, so start with the ones that are most gentle and won't stress a delicate little body. The chart on page 23 lists the best foods to introduce in the first couple of months. Raw fruits are the easiest to digest, but it's important to serve vegetables early on to help your baby move away from the sweet taste of breast milk, and so you don't encourage a sweet tooth. Don't fall into the cliché of 'kids don't like vegetables'. Children do like vegetables, just not every vegetable all the time and not overcooked, tasteless vegetables.

REACTIONS TO FOODS: Try one food at a time for a couple of days at first. If your baby doesn't seem to like it, simply try it again after a few weeks. With each food, see if there is any reaction, such as redness in the face, repeated sneezing or tummy upsets that cause diarrhoea or constipation. If there is a reaction to a food, wait eight weeks and then try again. Her system may be able to handle it later on.

HOW MUCH TO START?: At the beginning, she may eat only one or two spoonfuls at each meal, or she may eat a whole mashed banana. It doesn't matter. It depends on your baby. Give her as much as she'll eat. If she turns her head away or won't open her mouth after one mouthful or after ten, then stop. Put the food down and distract her with a rattle or a toy, then try again. Some babies eat and then need a little break before taking more. If she still won't eat more, just stop and try again at the next meal. Food is new to her and her stomach is tiny. She will gradually eat more – and you'll figure it out together. Just make sure she's getting enough breast milk or formula and trying a variety of foods each week, and she will thrive and change and start to grow up before your eyes.

Introducing foods in the sequence suggested in each chapter is the best way to ensure that your baby digests foods easily and thoroughly. Sometimes babies cry or get windy or doubled over from an upset tummy. Remember that they have the same length of intestines that we have, but theirs are crammed into a really tiny space. Eating and digesting is not always easy for them! If she is uncomfortable, gently rub your hand in a clockwise circle from her belly button downwards and back up to help

## FOODS TO BEGIN WITH AT 4–6 MONTHS

*Begin weaning your baby using the foods listed in the chart below. Remember to take it slowly to give your child a gentle transition to solid foods.*

| FRUITS* | VEGETABLES | GRAINS | PULSES | DAIRY & EGGS | FATS |
|---|---|---|---|---|---|
| *remove all skins<br><br>• apple (cooked or raw)<br>• apricot (fresh or dried)<br>• avocado (after four weeks)<br>• banana<br>• lemon juice, only for soaking pulses<br>• mango<br>• nectarine<br>• papaya<br>• peach<br>• pear<br>• plum (fresh or dried [prune]) | • artichoke heart<br>• beetroot<br>• broccoli<br>• butternut squash<br>• carrot<br>• cauliflower<br>• courgette<br>• green bean<br>• kombu, only for cooking pulses<br>• mangetout<br>• parsnip<br>• pea<br>• pumpkin<br>• swede<br>• sweet potato<br>• turnip | • amaranth<br>• brown rice<br>• millet<br>• quinoa<br>• white rice | • flageolet bean<br>• red lentil | • kefir, only for soaking grains<br>• yogurt, only for soaking grains | • Serve 1 teaspoon per day of cold-pressed seed oil mixed with food<br><br>Choose from:<br>flax<br>hemp<br>pumpkin<br>safflower<br>sesame<br>sunflower |

move things through her system. You can also try giving her cooled fennel tea in a bottle or by the spoonful to help ease digestion.

**IS SHE EATING ENOUGH?:** If a couple of months go by and you don't think she's eating enough, plot her weight on a baby weight chart and see if she is maintaining the same percentile. If she is, don't worry. If she isn't, talk to your doctor. But if your baby is happy, contented, sleeps well and doesn't cry much, then she is probably fine. If a baby is hungry, she will cry and keep on crying until you feed her.

**COMFORTABLE FEEDING:** If you're weaning your baby at four months, she won't be able to sit up in a chair, so feeding can be awkward. For effortless, intimate feeding at this age, sit on a soft chair or sofa and, if you're right handed, put your right foot flat on the floor and cross your left leg over and rest the ankle just above your right knee. Put your baby's bottom in the hole created by your left leg and she can lean back while she eats.

**RAW, STEAMED & PURÉED FOOD:** For this age, raw fruit should be puréed or mashed until very smooth, and dried fruit should be cooked until completely soft before puréeing. All other foods should be steamed (see page 17) until completely soft, then puréed. The puréed texture should be smooth and runny like yogurt, with no lumps, and the food should be served warm. Think of your baby's tummy as a little cauldron with a flame underneath that needs to be kept warm. If you serve cold food, her body wastes energy heating it up before she can begin to process it. You can freeze the purée you don't immediately need in ice-cube trays, and when they're frozen, pop them out into containers that you can label and date. Then just defrost the cubes and reheat them (see page 18).

You'll find that the purées in this chapter are incredibly easy to make. You don't have to worry about weighing or measuring out most ingredients because when you're steaming, puréeing and freezing a butternut squash, for example, it doesn't really matter how big the squash is. The more you cook at one time, though, the easier meals will be – as long as you have storage space in your freezer. I guarantee you will use everything you make. This means that most of the recipes in this chapter don't make a specific number of servings. How many meals a batch of Baby Brown Rice lasts really depends on how much your baby eats and how you eventually combine it with other ingredients.

If you're not sure where to start and you do have room in your freezer, I recommend making a selection of the recipes in this chapter. Dishes such as Butternut Squash Purée, Broccoli & Cauliflower Purée, Dried Apricot Purée, Baby Brown Rice Purée, Quinoa Purée, Flageolet Purée and Red Lentil Purée are good choices to begin with and will provide an impressive variety that you can mix and match as your baby starts to eat more.

Although the grain purées in this book are best, instant millet or brown rice flakes can be useful for thickening a meal if you accidentally water it down too much, or for mixing with jarred baby food when travelling to make a more substantial meal.

FATS: Once your baby starts weaning, give her some good-quality oil each day. Most people are deficient in essential fatty acids, which provide vital nutrients and aid brain and nerve development. Hemp oil is the only common seed oil that meets all known essential fatty acid needs, but other seed oils are also good. Add one teaspoon of cold-pressed oil to one meal each day. If your baby doesn't like the strong flavour of flax or hemp oil, you may find she's happier to take one of the milder seed oils, such as pumpkin, safflower or sesame.

If there is any history of seed allergies in your family, wait until your baby is at least fifteen months old to introduce seeds and seed oils, and watch for any reaction.

## MEAL PLANNER FOR BABIES AT 4–6 MONTHS

*Use these general guidelines to help you plan your baby's weaning schedule. Remember to take it slowly – every child is different and will want to transition to solid food at a different pace.*

### WEEKS 1 AND 2

| BREAKFAST | MID-MORNING | LUNCH | MID-AFTERNOON | TEA | EVENING |
|---|---|---|---|---|---|
| breast/bottle | breast/bottle | breast/bottle<br>one fruit or vegetable<br>1 tsp seed oil<br>In week 2, add Baby Brown Rice Purée (see page 30) | breast/bottle | one fruit or vegetable | breast/bottle |

### FROM WEEK 3

| BREAKFAST | MID-MORNING | LUNCH | MID-AFTERNOON | TEA | EVENING |
|---|---|---|---|---|---|
| breast/bottle<br>Baby Brown Rice Purée (see page 30)<br>or Millet Purée (see page 33)<br>one fruit<br>1 tsp seed oil | breast/bottle | breast/bottle<br>one vegetable<br>one bean | breast/bottle | breast/bottle<br>Quinoa Purée (see page 33)<br>or Amaranth Purée (see page 32)<br>one vegetable | breast/bottle |

# apple purée

PREPARATION TIME:
5 minutes

STORAGE:
Refrigerate for up to 3 days or freeze cubes of the purée for up to 3 months.

Raw fruit is the easiest food for your baby to digest – and it is packed with living nutrition. You can also use this recipe for apricot, mango, nectarine, papaya, peach, pear or plum purée. Each fruit is great on its own as a snack or mixed with a grain purée for a healthy breakfast.

**1 apple, peeled, cored and chopped**

**1** Put the apple in a blender and blend for 1 minute until smooth, adding a little water if the mixture is too dry.

**2** Serve immediately to prevent the apple discolouring.

*apples* are so common that we often overlook them. Don't! They combine antioxidants, flavanoids and fibre in a way that's superior to other fruits. Much of the goodness is in the skin. Peel them now, but leave the skin on once your baby can chew it – around nine months.

# dried apricot purée

PREPARATION TIME:
3 minutes, plus overnight soaking

COOKING TIME:
15 minutes

STORAGE:
Refrigerate for up to 3 days or freeze cubes of the cooled purée for up to 3 months.

Apricots sweeten food in a nutritious way and are a good source of beta-carotene. You can use prunes for this recipe, too. It's good to have some of these dense purées to hand as ice cubes that you can quickly defrost and serve warm when hunger suddenly strikes.

**175g/6oz/1 cup unsulphured dried apricots**

**1** Put the apricots and 350ml/12fl oz/scant 1½ cups water in a small saucepan and leave to soak, covered, overnight.

**2** Bring the apricots and soaking water to the boil over a high heat, then reduce the heat to low and simmer, covered, for 15 minutes, stirring occasionally, until completely soft. If using a blender with a plastic container, leave the mixture to cool completely before blending.

**3** Transfer the mixture to a blender and blend for 1 minute until smooth. Serve warm, reheating if necessary.

# ▲ banana mash

**MAKES:**
1 serving

**PREPARATION TIME:**
3 minutes

**STORAGE:**
Use immediately. Not suitable for storage.

My daughter Cassie couldn't get enough of this mash. Banana makes a great emergency food, especially if your baby wakes up hungry at night.

**1 banana, peeled**

**1** Put the banana on a plate and mash, using a fork, until it forms a smooth paste, adding a little water if necessary. For a smoother consistency, chop the banana into pieces, put it in a blender and blend for 1 minute, adding a little water if necessary, until smooth.

**2** Serve immediately to prevent the banana discolouring.

*bananas* are one of nature's best sources of potassium, which helps to regulate salt in the body. The potassium in bananas is also particularly valuable when your baby has diarrhoea. Their pectin content, on the other hand, can help to relieve constipation.

# avocado mash

Probably the healthiest fruit, avocado is satisfying, nourishing and easy to digest. It also contains the best fat you can give your little one. It's been one of my daughter Jessie's favourites since she was tiny.

MAKES:
1 serving

PREPARATION TIME:
3 minutes

STORAGE:
Use immediately. Not suitable for storage.

½ avocado, pitted

1 Scoop the avocado flesh into a blender and add enough warm water to cover halfway.
2 Blend for 1 minute until smooth, adding more water if necessary. Serve immediately to prevent the avocado discolouring.

*avocados* are so packed with nutrition that they can be thought of as a complete food. They are full of fibre, potassium and B vitamins, as well as important monounsaturated fatty acids, which may help boost memory.

# artichoke heart purée

This lovely purée is a nice way to introduce your baby to artichokes. Add them in small quantities to other dishes until your baby is a toddler, and old enough to enjoy them roasted or baked.

PREPARATION TIME:
10 minutes

COOKING TIME:
45 minutes

STORAGE:
Refrigerate for up to 3 days or freeze cubes of the cooled purée for up to 3 months.

2 globe artichokes, stems removed

1 Put the artichokes in a steamer and steam, covered, over boiling water for 45 minutes until a leaf pulled from the top comes out easily. Add extra boiling water during steaming if necessary. Remove from the heat and set aside until cool enough to handle, reserving the steam water.

2 Peel the leaves off the artichokes and reserve them to serve as a starter for yourself dipped in olive oil or melted butter. Using a sharp knife, carefully cut out and discard the hairy chokes, then chop the artichoke hearts and transfer them to a blender (leaving them to cool completely first if using a blender with a plastic container). Add enough of the reserved steam water to cover the artichoke hearts halfway. Blend for 1 minute until smooth. Serve warm, reheating if necessary.

# carrot purée

You can use vegetables like peas, courgettes and unpeeled parsnips and sweet potatoes in this recipe, although you'll need to watch cooking times and reduce the time for courgettes (15 minutes) and peas (7 minutes).

PREPARATION TIME:
10 minutes

COOKING TIME:
25 minutes

STORAGE:
Refrigerate for up to 3 days or freeze cubes of the cooled purée for up to 3 months.

**6 carrots, unpeeled, but topped and tailed**

**1** Cut the carrots in half lengthways and then into 2.5cm/1in pieces. Put them in a steamer and steam, covered, over boiling water for 20–25 minutes until completely soft. Reserve the steam water. If using a blender with a plastic container, leave the carrots to cool completely before blending.

**2** Transfer the carrots to a blender and add enough of the steam water to cover them halfway. Blend for 1 minute until smooth. Serve warm, reheating if necessary.

# broccoli & cauliflower purée

You can cook these separately but mixing them together makes a great combination. Save the broccoli stalk for yourself: simply cut off the hard skin and enjoy the sweet centre raw or lightly steamed.

PREPARATION TIME:
10 minutes

COOKING TIME:
10 minutes

STORAGE:
Refrigerate for up to 3 days or freeze cubes of the cooled purée for up to 3 months.

**100g/3½oz broccoli, cut into 3cm/1¼in florets
100g/3½oz cauliflower, cut into 3cm/1¼in florets**

**1** Put the broccoli and cauliflower in a steamer and steam, covered, over boiling water for 10 minutes, or until completely soft. Reserve the steam water. If using a blender with a plastic container, leave the vegetables to cool completely before blending.

**2** Transfer the vegetables to a blender and add enough of the steam water to cover them halfway. Blend for 1 minute until smooth. Serve warm, reheating if necessary.

# butternut squash purée ▶

Pumpkin and squash are my favourite first vegetables. They have a lovely sweetness and are easily digested by delicate little stomachs. Use this recipe for beetroot, green beans, mangetout and peeled swede and turnip, too.

**PREPARATION TIME:**
10 minutes

**COOKING TIME:**
30 minutes

**STORAGE:** Refrigerate for up to 3 days or freeze cubes of the cooled purée for up to 3 months.

**1 butternut squash, peeled, deseeded and cut into 5cm/2in squares**

**1** Put the squash in a steamer and steam, covered, over boiling water for 30 minutes until completely soft. Reserve the steam water. If using a blender with a plastic container, leave the squash to cool completely before blending.

**2** Transfer the squash to a blender and add enough of the steam water to cover it halfway. Blend for 1 minute until smooth. Serve warm, reheating if necessary.

*butternut squash* is sweet, filling and incredibly versatile. Its lovely hue comes from its beta-carotene content, which rivals even that of mangoes and cantaloupe.

# baby brown rice purée

Many parents buy white rice or brown rice flakes, but your baby gets much better nutrition when you make your own brown rice purée.

**PREPARATION TIME:**
5 minutes, plus at least 7 hours soaking

**COOKING TIME:**
1 hour

**STORAGE:** Refrigerate for up to 1 day or freeze cubes of the cooled purée for up to 1 month. Reheat until hot.

**100g/3½oz/½ cup brown basmati rice**
**1 tsp kefir or natural yogurt**

**1** Put the rice, kefir and 570ml/20fl oz/scant 2⅓ cups warm water in a medium saucepan and leave to soak, covered, for 7 hours or overnight.

**2** Bring to the boil over a high heat, then reduce the heat to low and simmer, covered, for 1 hour until the rice is very tender. If using a blender with a plastic container, leave the rice to cool completely before blending.

**3** Transfer the rice to a blender and blend for 1 minute until smooth. Serve warm, reheating if necessary.

*kefir* is a fermented milk product that contains beneficial bacteria and yeast cultures, which aid digestion and promote the development of good probiotic flora in the gut.

## ▲ amaranth purée

Variety is so important in a baby's diet. Adding amaranth into your rotation of grains gives you choice and a new mix of minerals and vitamins. It has a lovely flavour and can be combined with anything.

PREPARATION TIME:
5 minutes, plus at least 7 hours soaking

COOKING TIME:
40 minutes

STORAGE:
Refrigerate for up to 3 days or freeze cubes of the cooled purée for up to 3 months.

**100g/3½oz/½ cup amaranth**
**1 tsp kefir or natural yogurt**

**1** Put the amaranth, kefir and 455ml/16fl oz/scant 2 cups warm water in a medium saucepan and leave to soak, covered, for 7 hours or overnight.

**2** Bring to the boil over a high heat, then reduce the heat to low and cook, covered, for 40 minutes, stirring occasionally so it doesn't clump to the bottom of the pan. If using a blender with a plastic container, leave the amaranth to cool completely before blending.

**3** Transfer the amaranth to a blender and blend for 1 minute until smooth. Serve warm, reheating if necessary.

# millet purée

Millet is a slightly bitter grain. Try it first with non-sweet vegetables and if your baby doesn't like it, try it with either sweet vegetables or fruits.

PREPARATION TIME:
5 minutes, plus at least 7 hours soaking

COOKING TIME:
45 minutes

STORAGE:
Refrigerate for up to 3 days or freeze cubes of the cooled purée for up to 3 months.

**100g/3½oz/½ cup millet**
**1 tsp kefir or natural yogurt**

**1** Put the millet, kefir and 700ml/24fl oz/2¾ cups warm water in a medium saucepan and leave to soak, covered, for 7 hours or overnight.

**2** Bring to the boil over a high heat. Skim any scum that rises to the surface, then reduce the heat to low and simmer, covered, for 45 minutes until completely soft. If using a blender with a plastic container, leave the millet to cool completely before blending.

**3** Transfer the millet to a blender and blend for 1 minute until smooth. Serve warm, reheating if necessary.

*millet* is one of the oldest foods known and possibly the first cereal grain used. It is alkaline and helps balance acidity in the body. It is also easy to digest, helps bowel function and is calming.

# quinoa purée

Quinoa, the highest protein grain, is an excellent grain to add to your repertoire and adds variety to your baby's diet. Quinoa must be soaked, as in this recipe, or toasted as in the recipe on page 47 before cooking.

PREPARATION TIME:
5 minutes, plus at least 7 hours soaking

COOKING TIME:
40 minutes

STORAGE:
Refrigerate for up to 3 days or freeze cubes of the cooled purée for up to 3 months.

**85g/3oz/½ cup quinoa**
**1 tsp kefir or natural yogurt**

**1** Put the quinoa, kefir and 400ml/14fl oz/1⅔ cups warm water in a medium saucepan and leave to soak, covered, for 7 hours or overnight.

**2** Bring to the boil over a high heat, then reduce the heat to low and simmer, covered, for 40 minutes until the quinoa is very tender. If using a blender with a plastic container, leave the quinoa to cool completely before blending.

**3** Transfer the quinoa to a blender and blend for 1 minute until smooth. Serve warm, reheating if necessary.

# white rice purée

PREPARATION TIME:
5 minutes

COOKING TIME:
30 minutes

STORAGE:
Refrigerate for up to 1 day or freeze cubes of the cooled purée for up to 1 month. Reheat until hot.

I always prefer whole grains, but white rice is the least allergenic food and is very gentle on the digestive tract. It's ideal if your little one has had an upset tummy – or has a medical reason not to eat whole grains.

100g/3½oz/½ cup white basmati rice

1 Put the rice and 400ml/14fl oz/1⅔ cups water in a medium saucepan, cover and bring to the boil over a high heat. Reduce the heat to low and cook for 30 minutes until very soft. If using a blender with a plastic container, leave the rice to cool completely before blending.

2 Transfer the rice to a blender and blend for 1 minute until smooth. Serve warm, reheating if necessary.

# red lentil purée

PREPARATION TIME:
5 minutes, plus overnight soaking

COOKING TIME:
55 minutes

STORAGE:
Refrigerate for up to 3 days or freeze cubes of the cooled purée for up to 3 months.

Lentils are easy to digest and add protein to a meal. They're a great staple to have in your freezer to bulk up baby meals. Use up to three frozen cubes mixed with rice and vegetables.

100g/3½oz/½ cup split red lentils
2 tsp lemon juice

1 Put the lentils and lemon juice in a medium saucepan, cover with water and leave to soak, covered, overnight.

2 Drain and rinse the lentils. Return them to the pan, add 455ml/16fl oz/scant 2 cups water and bring to the boil for 10 minutes over a high heat, skimming any scum that rises to the surface. Reduce the heat to low and cook, covered, for 45 minutes until completely soft. If using a blender with a plastic container, leave the mixture to cool completely before blending.

3 Transfer the lentils and cooking liquid to a blender and blend for 1 minute until smooth. Serve warm, reheating if necessary.

*red lentils* are nutritional giants packed with protein, high amounts of six minerals and two B vitamins. Their high fibre content prevents blood sugar levels from rising quickly.

# ▼ flageolet purée

Cooking pulses with kombu, a vitamin- and mineral-packed seaweed, helps make them more easily digestible, especially for tiny tummies.

**PREPARATION TIME:**
5 minutes, plus overnight soaking

**COOKING TIME:**
2 hours 10 minutes

**STORAGE:**
Refrigerate for up to 3 days or freeze cubes of the cooled purée for up to 3 months.

**85g/3oz/½ cup dried flageolet beans**
**2 tsp lemon juice**
**1 strip of kombu, about 8 x 5cm/3¼ x 2in**

**1** Put the beans and lemon juice in a medium saucepan, cover with water and leave to soak, covered, overnight.

**2** Drain and rinse the beans. Return them to the pan and add 570ml/20fl oz/scant 2⅓ cups water. Bring to the boil over a high heat and boil for 10 minutes, skimming any scum that rises to the surface. Reduce the heat to low, add the kombu and cook, covered, for 2 hours until completely soft, then discard the kombu. If using a blender with a plastic container, leave the mixture to cool completely before blending.

**3** Transfer the beans and cooking liquid to a blender and blend for 1 minute until smooth, adding a little more water if necessary. Serve warm, reheating if necessary.

# three meals a day

If you've waited for your baby to reach six months before weaning, follow chapter 1 before advancing to the recipes in this chapter. If he's already getting used to eating from a spoon, it's time to make things even more interesting by combining flavours. His digestive system is ready for lots of new foods, too. Although he's still consuming breast milk or formula, a good percentage of his calories is now coming from other foods – so high-quality protein is important. A bigger variety of pulses and the introduction of fish, poultry and meat make it easy to create exciting meals. Quinoa & Coconut Porridge, succulent Sardines & Sweet Potato and savoury-sweet Haricot Beans with Beetroot are just a few new options. Try mixing and matching different foods, too – you might stumble upon a combination that he'll absolutely love.

*Haricot Beans & Beetroot (see page 46)*

# 6 to 9 months

If your baby hasn't started weaning yet, six months is the time to start. Begin with chapter 1 first and then start introducing the foods in this chapter.

Your baby's first teeth may have already appeared, and if they haven't, they will soon. Either way, he's probably showing a much greater interest in chewing now. At this stage, his food should still be puréed, but you can gradually start to leave it a little lumpier by puréeing for a shorter time or simply mashing it with a fork. If you give your baby lumpier food and he starts pooping out lumps, go back to smoother purées until he's chewing more. Don't worry if he isn't chewing yet. It will just happen later, when he's ready.

**GRATED FOOD & FOOD PIECES:** Once he is chewing lumps, you can start introducing some exciting new textures by mixing finely grated raw fruits and vegetables into his food. This will encourage him to chew more – without the risk of choking. Because you're grating fruit so finely, you can also start to include the skins, which have great nutritional value. Along with the lumpier purées, you can now offer your baby little pieces, about 5mm/¼in in size, of well-cooked vegetables or soft raw fruit (without skins), too. Not only does this encourage him to chew, it also encourages him to feed himself. He can start munching on tiny bits at the table while you are cooking or heating up the main course.

If your baby is just starting to chew, let him try some puffed rice. It's small, dissolves in the mouth easily and is good for hand-eye coordination. If your baby is teething and chewing well, and you want to give him something to really chew on, start with unsalted brown rice cakes. They're healthy, and they disintegrate easily. Avoid commercially available rusks, which are made of white flour and sugar and have little nutritional value.

**CONTINUING WITH BREAST MILK OR FORMULA:** Your baby will now be having three good meals each day, but you should carry on giving him breast milk or formula at breakfast and between meals because it's still an important source of protein for him. Give him as much solid food as he'll eat at breakfast first and then finish the meal off with some breast milk or formula. Between meals, when he isn't having solid foods, let him take as much breast milk as he wants; if you're giving him formula instead, follow the instructions on the packet to determine how much is appropriate for this age.

**DRINKS:** Now that he's having his milk between meals and the purées are becoming more substantial and less watery, you can start to offer a little water at mealtimes. Unless you have well water and don't live an area where intensive agriculture is leaching chemicals into your well, I suggest filtering tap water to remove the worst of the chemicals and unwanted metals that may be in there. Make sure to serve his water slightly warm so it doesn't chill the stomach. Drinking water is a great habit to get your child into, and it's one of the healthiest drinks you can give him.

I don't offer diluted fruit juices because I think the nutritional benefit is minimal – he's much better off eating puréed or mashed fruit instead. Most babies are attracted to anything sweet, but this can lead to a sugar addiction (see page 14), which is hard for anyone to break. You also don't want his stomach to fill up with sweet juice instead of food. When he's older, you might want to give him juice as an occasional treat, but at this age it's best to focus on making sure his calories come from nutritious whole foods.

## NEW FOODS TO INTRODUCE AT 6–9 MONTHS
*Your child is now ready for the foods listed in the chart below. Combine them with the foods listed in the previous chapter to give him the best variety you can.*

| GRAINS | PULSES | NUTS & SEEDS | FISH | POULTRY & MEATS* | FATS |
|---|---|---|---|---|---|
| • buckwheat | • black bean<br>• black-eyed bean<br>• broad bean (no skins)<br>• cannellini bean<br>• chickpea<br>• haricot bean<br>• lentil, including brown, green and Puy<br>• mung bean<br>• pinto bean | • coconut | • anchovy (fresh not tinned)<br>• mackerel<br>• salmon<br>• sardine | * Serve all poultry and meats in small amounts only<br><br>• beef and other red meats<br>• poultry<br>• venison and other game | • olive oil |

**PROTEIN:** Your baby is growing and developing quickly, so protein is becoming more important now, especially as he begins reducing the amount of milk he drinks. His digestive system is getting used to more foods and is ready for slightly heavier ones such as fish and meats, which are great sources of protein. I try to give different proteins three times a day, but if I manage it only twice, that's okay.

**FISH:** You can now introduce fish, which can be an excellent source of essential fatty acids. Be aware, however, that many kinds of fish carry toxins, including dioxins and polychlorinated biphenyls (PCBs), from the poisons that we dump into our waterways. So the lower down the food chain you eat the better. By this I mean, eat small fish instead of big fish. Small fish that eat plankton accumulate far fewer toxins in their flesh than large carnivorous fish, such as tuna, that eat lots and lots of little fish and, as a result, build up more toxins. The best fish to eat are fresh anchovies (not tinned ones because they're too salty) and any sardines. These are also good because their tiny, soft bones provide calcium but pose no choking risk. Avoid conventionally farmed fish, which is raised in poor, crowded conditions. Some varieties of organic fish are available. Although they must be farmed in order to maintain organic standards, they are raised in the best environment and given the best feed possible, so this is the only farmed fish worth eating. Look for sustainably sourced seafood, too, which is caught using methods that have a less severe impact on the ecosystem. Suppliers of sustainably fished seafood do not deplete already-threatened populations of fish, trap unwanted fish and dolphins in vast nets or trawl the ocean floor, causing irreparable damage. They are good alternatives to overfished varieties. Try pollock and haddock, for example, instead of overfished cod.

**POULTRY & MEAT:** You can also introduce poultry and meat. Organic poultry and red meats are, without question, the best because they do not contain growth hormones or antibiotic residues. Game is next best because it is wild, lean and not subjected to the unpleasantries of conventional farming practices. If organic meat doesn't suit your budget, buy a little when you can and then provide protein through grain and bean combinations. Remember that variety is always the best policy anyway, and eating less meat is better not only for human health but for the health of our environment. Make sure that poultry and meats are completely cooked to avoid any problems with bacteria.

**COCONUT:** Coconut has good fats and provides a new texture and delicious flavour. Wait, however, until 15–24 months to introduce other nuts and seeds. As always, watch for any reaction in your child. If there is one, wait eight weeks and then try again.

**FATS:** Continue adding two teaspoons of cold-pressed oil to your baby's food each day – or feed it to him by the teaspoonful if he'll take it. His brain and nervous system are still developing, and the essential fats in these oils are extremely important.

# MEAL PLANNER FOR BABIES AT 6–9 MONTHS

*This planner ensures that your baby eats a mixture of grains, fruits and vegetables each day and through the week. Breast milk or formula still provides good protein.*

| DAY | BREAKFAST | MID-MORNING | LUNCH | MID-AFTERNOON | TEA | EVENING |
|---|---|---|---|---|---|---|
| 1 | Millet Purée (see page 33) Apple Purée (see page 26) with 2 tsp seed oil breast/bottle | breast/bottle | Baby Brown Rice Purée (see page 30) Avocado Mash (see page 28) warm water | breast/bottle | Sardines & Sweet Potato (see page 49) warm water | breast/bottle |
| 2 | Amaranth Purée (see page 32) Dried Apricot Purée (see page 26) with 2 tsp seed oil breast/bottle | breast/bottle | Buckwheat & Carrot (see page 43) with 2 tsp olive oil warm water | breast/bottle | Beef & Cauliflower (see page 50) warm water | breast/bottle |
| 3 | Quinoa & Coconut Porridge (see page 42) pear purée (see Apple Purée on page 26) with 2 tsp seed oil breast/bottle | breast/bottle | Puy Lentils & Butternut Squash (see page 43) with 2 tsp olive oil warm water | breast/bottle | Mackerel & Broccoli (see page 49) warm water | breast/bottle |
| 4 | Rice & Mango Breakfast (see page 42) with 2 tsp seed oil breast/bottle | breast/bottle | Haricot Beans & Beetroot (see page 46) with 2 tsp olive oil warm water | breast/bottle | Chicken & Courgette (see page 51) warm water | breast/bottle |
| 5 | Millet Purée (see page 33) Banana Mash (see page 27) with 2 tsp seed oil breast/bottle | breast/bottle | Mung Beans with Toasted Quinoa (see page 47) with 2 tsp olive oil warm water | breast/bottle | Venison & Parsnip (see page 50) warm water | breast/bottle |
| 6 | Quinoa Purée (see page 33) papaya purée (see Apple Purée on page 26) breast/bottle | breast/bottle | Broad Bean & Pumpkin Purée (see page 45) with 2 tsp seed oil warm water | breast/bottle | Black-Eyed Beans & Brown Rice (see page 45) with 2 tsp olive oil warm water | breast/bottle |
| 7 | Baby Brown Rice Purée (see page 30) plum purée (see Apple Purée on page 26) with 2 tsp seed oil breast/bottle | breast/bottle | Pinto Beans, Millet & Avocado (see page 44) warm water | breast/bottle | Salmon & Peas (see page 48) warm water | breast/bottle |

# quinoa & coconut porridge

Porridge is made not only with oats. Remember amaranth, brown rice, buckwheat, millet and quinoa when you need creative breakfast ideas.

MAKES:
2 servings

PREPARATION TIME:
5 minutes, plus overnight soaking and making the apricot purée

COOKING TIME:
40 minutes

STORAGE:
Refrigerate for up to 3 days or freeze cubes of the cooled purée for up to 3 months.

**85g/3oz/½ cup quinoa**
**2 tbsp flaked coconut**
**1 tbsp kefir or natural yogurt**
**2 tsp Dried Apricot Purée (see page 26), to serve**

1 Put the quinoa, coconut, kefir and 350ml/12fl oz/scant 1½ cups warm water in a medium saucepan and leave to soak, covered, overnight.

2 Bring the mixture to the boil over a high heat, then reduce the heat to low and simmer, covered, for 40 minutes until the quinoa is very soft. If using a blender with a plastic container, leave the mixture to cool completely before blending.

3 Transfer the mixture to a blender and blend for 1 minute until smooth. Serve warm with the apricot purée, reheating if necessary.

# rice & mango breakfast

This is one of Nicholas's favourite breakfasts. The brown rice flakes are a wonderful alternative to porridge oats. They cook more quickly than brown rice, making this delicious dish perfect for mornings when you're pushed for time.

MAKES:
4 servings

PREPARATION TIME:
10 minutes, plus overnight soaking

COOKING TIME:
10 minutes

STORAGE:
Refrigerate the mango purée for up to 3 days or freeze in cubes for up to 3 months. Refrigerate the cooled porridge for up to 1 day. Reheat until hot.

**55g/2oz/½ cup brown rice flakes**
**1 tbsp kefir or natural yogurt**
**1 mango, peeled, pitted and chopped**
**¼ apple, peeled and grated, to serve**

1 Put the rice flakes, kefir and 185ml/6fl oz/¾ cup warm water in a medium saucepan and leave to soak, covered, overnight.

2 Bring the mixture to a simmer over a medium heat, then reduce the heat to low and cook for 10 minutes, stirring occasionally, until the rice flakes are very soft.

3 Meanwhile, put the mango in a blender and blend for 1 minute until smooth. Stir the puréed mango into the porridge, then sprinkle with the grated apple. Serve warm.

*mango*
is high in iron, vitamin E, beta-carotene and selenium. It's a deliciously sweet fruit that's great for aiding digestion and balancing acidity in the body.

# buckwheat & carrot

Buckwheat's strong flavour is balanced here by sweet carrot. Some babies will love this on its own as a main course; others will prefer it as a side dish.

MAKES:
4 servings

PREPARATION TIME:
5 minutes, plus at least 7 hours soaking

COOKING TIME:
25 minutes

STORAGE:
Refrigerate for up to 3 days or freeze cubes of the cooled purée for up to 3 months.

**2 tbsp buckwheat**
**1 tsp kefir or natural yogurt**
**1 carrot, quartered lengthways and cut into 5mm/¼in pieces**

**1** Put the buckwheat, kefir and 185ml/6fl oz/¾ cup warm water in a small saucepan and leave to soak, covered, at room temperature for at least 7 hours or overnight.

**2** Add the carrot, cover, and bring to the boil over a high heat. Reduce the heat to low and simmer, covered, for 25 minutes. Leave to cool slightly, then serve warm. If desired, transfer the mixture to a blender (leaving the mixture to cool completely before blending if using a blender with a plastic container), then blend for 1 minute until smooth before serving warm, reheating if necessary.

# puy lentils & butternut squash

This beautiful combination of savoury lentils and naturally sweet butternut squash is sure to become a favourite with your baby.

MAKES:
4 servings

PREPARATION TIME:
10 minutes, plus overnight soaking

COOKING TIME:
1 hour 5 minutes

STORAGE:
Refrigerate for up to 3 days or freeze cubes of the cooled purée for up to 3 months.

**100g/3½oz/½ cup Puy lentils**
**2 tsp lemon juice**
**1 small butternut squash, peeled, deseeded and cut into 2.5cm/1in square chunks**
**1 tbsp olive oil**

**1** Put the lentils and lemon juice in a medium saucepan, cover with warm water and leave to soak, covered, overnight.

**2** Drain and rinse the lentils. Return them to the pan and add 375ml/13fl oz/1½ cups water. Bring to the boil over a high heat and boil for 10 minutes, skimming any scum that rises to the surface. Reduce the heat to low and cook, covered, for 1 hour until completely soft.

**3** Meanwhile, preheat the oven to 200°C/400°F/Gas 6. Put the squash in a shallow baking dish, drizzle with the olive oil and toss to coat. Bake for 30–40 minutes until very soft and lightly browned. Remove from the oven. If using a blender with a plastic container, leave the squash and lentils to cool completely before blending.

**4** Transfer the squash, lentils and cooking liquid to a blender. Blend for 1 minute until smooth. Serve warm, reheating if necessary.

# ▲ pinto beans, millet & avocado

I love avocado with anything. Serving it with creamy pinto beans makes it a more substantial meal for your growing baby.

**MAKES:**
4 servings

**PREPARATION TIME:**
5 minutes, plus overnight soaking and making the avocado and millet

**COOKING TIME:**
2 hours 10 minutes

**STORAGE:**
Refrigerate for up to 3 days or freeze cubes of the cooled bean purée for up to 3 months.

40g/1½oz/¼ cup dried pinto beans
2 tsp lemon juice
1 strip of kombu, about 8 x 5cm/3¼ x 2in
1 recipe quantity Avocado Mash (see page 28)
4 portions Millet Purée (see page 33)

**1** Put the beans and lemon juice in a medium saucepan, cover with warm water and leave to soak, covered, overnight.

**2** Drain and rinse the beans. Return them to the pan and add 290ml/10fl oz/scant 1¼ cups water. Bring to the boil over a high heat and boil for 10 minutes, skimming any scum that rises to the surface. Reduce the heat to low, add the kombu and cook, covered, for 2 hours until the beans are completely soft, then discard the kombu. If using a blender with a plastic container, leave the mixture to cool completely before blending.

**3** Transfer the mixture to a blender and blend for 1 minute until smooth. Serve warm with the avocado mash and millet purée, or mix all three purées together, reheating the millet and beans if necessary.

# broad bean & pumpkin purée

Sweet pumpkin goes well with anything, combined with fresh broad beans, it's simply amazing. Broad beans are a particularly special treat when they're in season because they're so fresh.

**MAKES:**
4 servings

**PREPARATION TIME:**
10 minutes, plus making the pumpkin purée

**COOKING TIME:**
10 minutes

**STORAGE:**
Refrigerate for up to 3 days or freeze cubes of the cooled bean purée for up to 3 months.

**16 broad bean pods**
**2 portions pumpkin purée (see Butternut Squash Purée, page 30)**

1 Slit each bean pod along its seam and pop the beans out. Bring a small saucepan of water to the boil over a high heat, add the beans and boil for 10 minutes until soft. Remove from the heat, drain and leave to cool, then peel the beans and discard the tough skins.

2 Transfer the beans to a blender and add enough water to cover halfway. Blend for 1 minute until smooth.

3 Put the pumpkin purée and 1–2 tablespoons water in a saucepan and heat over a medium heat until warm, then stir in the broad bean purée. Serve warm.

# black-eyed beans & brown rice

A classic vegetarian protein, the combination of beans and rice forms a complete protein that has all the essential amino acids the body needs.

**MAKES:**
4 servings

**PREPARATION TIME:**
5 minutes, plus overnight soaking and making the brown rice purée

**COOKING TIME:**
2 hours 10 minutes

**STORAGE:**
Refrigerate for up to 1 day or freeze cubes of the cooled bean purée for up to 3 months.

**85g/3oz/½ cup dried black-eyed beans**
**2 tsp lemon juice**
**1 strip of kombu, about 8 x 5cm/3¼ x 2in**
**4 portions Baby Brown Rice Purée (see page 30)**

1 Put the beans and lemon juice in a medium saucepan, cover with warm water and leave to soak, covered, overnight.

2 Drain and rinse the beans. Return them to the pan and add 570ml/20fl oz/scant 2⅓ cups water. Bring to the boil over a high heat and boil for 10 minutes, skimming any scum that rises to the surface. Reduce the heat to low, add the kombu and cook, covered, for 2 hours until the beans are completely soft, then discard the kombu. If using a blender with a plastic container, leave the mixture to cool completely before blending.

3 Transfer the mixture to a blender and blend for 1 minute until smooth. Serve warm with the rice, reheating if necessary.

# haricot beans & beetroot

Beetroot's natural sweetness beautifully complements haricot beans. This is a good dish to have as a side dish or to mix with a grain, such as quinoa or millet, to make a main dish.

MAKES:
4 servings

PREPARATION
TIME:
10 minutes, plus
overnight soaking

COOKING TIME:
1 hour 40 minutes

STORAGE:
Refrigerate for
up to 3 days or
freeze cubes of the
cooled purées for
up to 3 months.

**85g/3oz/½ cup dried
haricot beans**
**2 tsp lemon juice**
**1 strip of kombu, about
8 x 5cm/3¼ x 2in**
**4 small beetroot with
stalks, washed well
without breaking the
skin, stalks trimmed
to 2.5cm/1in**

**1** Put the beans and lemon juice in a medium saucepan, cover with warm water and leave to soak, covered, overnight.

**2** Drain and rinse the beans. Return them to the pan and add 570ml/20fl oz/scant 2⅓ cups water. Bring to the boil over a high heat and boil for 10 minutes, skimming any scum that rises to the top. Reduce the heat to low, add the kombu and cook, covered, for 1½ hours until the beans are completely soft, then discard the kombu. If using a blender with a plastic container, leave the mixture to cool completely before blending.

**3** Meanwhile, bring a medium saucepan of water to the boil over a high heat and add the beetroot, ensuring they are completely covered in water. Reduce the heat to low and simmer, covered, for 45 minutes until the beetroot are completely soft and the skins come off easily. Drain and leave to stand until cool enough to handle.

**4** Remove and discard the skins, then chop the beetroot, put them in a blender and blend for 1 minute until smooth, adding a little water if necessary. Transfer the purée to a bowl and wash the blender.

**5** Transfer the beans and cooking liquid to the blender and blend for 1 minute until smooth.

**6** Mix together equal quantities of the bean and beetroot purées. Serve warm, reheating if necessary

*beetroot*
contains silica,
which helps the body use
calcium. This is important for
your growing child's musculo-
skeletal development and
health. Beetroot also contains
high amounts of carotenoids
and flavanoids, which
are important
anti-oxidants.

# mung beans with toasted quinoa

Mung beans are easily digested, so they're perfect for your baby. Combining beans and grains is a wonderful way to get protein, so mix and match different combinations to create a range of healthy meals.

**MAKES:**
4 servings

**PREPARATION TIME:**
5 minutes, plus overnight soaking

**COOKING TIME:**
1 hour 10 minutes

**STORAGE:**
Refrigerate for up to 3 days or freeze cubes of the cooled purées for up to 3 months.

85g/3oz/½ cup dried mung beans
2 tsp lemon juice
1 strip of kombu, about 8 x 5cm/3¼ x 2in
85g/3oz/½ cup quinoa

**1** Put the beans and lemon juice in a medium saucepan, cover with warm water and leave to soak, covered, overnight.

**2** Drain and rinse the beans. Return them to the pan and add 570ml/20fl oz/scant 2⅓ cups water. Bring to the boil over a high heat and boil for 10 minutes, skimming any scum that rises to the surface. Reduce the heat to low, add the kombu and cook, covered, for 1 hour until the beans are completely soft, then discard the kombu.

**3** While the beans are cooking, put the quinoa in a sieve and rinse under cold running water, then drain well. Transfer to a medium saucepan and toast over a high heat for 5 minutes, stirring continuously, until any excess water has evaporated and the quinoa has browned slightly and begun to pop. Slowly add 240ml/8fl oz/scant 1 cup water, cover and bring to the boil over a high heat. Reduce the heat to low and simmer for 30 minutes until tender. If using a blender with a plastic container, leave both the quinoa and the bean mixture to cool completely before blending.

**4** Transfer the bean mixture to the blender and blend for 1 minute until smooth. Transfer the purée to a bowl and wash the blender.

**5** Put the quinoa in the blender and blend for 1 minute until smooth.

**6** Mix together equal quantities of the bean and quinoa purées. Serve warm, reheating if necessary.

*mung beans*
are known as the green or golden gram. They are sweet, soft and easily digestible. Low in fat, they are rich in carbohydrates and vitamins B1 and B2. Like all beans, they provide satiating bulk as your baby's appetite for solid food grows.

# ▲ salmon & peas

If you can get them, wild salmon and organic salmon are much better than conventionally farmed fish. The peas give this dish an intense sweetness.

**MAKES:**
4 servings

**PREPARATION TIME:**
5 minutes

**COOKING TIME:**
15 minutes

**STORAGE:**
Refrigerate for up to 2 days or freeze cubes of the cooled purée for up to 1 month.

2 tsp olive oil
115g/4oz salmon fillet, rinsed
4 tbsp peas

**1** Heat a small frying pan over a medium heat. Add the olive oil and when it is hot, add the salmon, skin-side up. Cook, covered, for 5 minutes, then turn the fish over. Cook, covered, for a further 5–10 minutes until cooked through. Meanwhile, put the peas in a steamer and steam, covered, over boiling water for 10 minutes until soft.

**2** When the fish has finished cooking, remove it from the heat. Remove and discard the skin and roughly chop the salmon, checking with your fingers for bones. If using a blender with a plastic container, leave both the peas and salmon to cool completely before blending.

**3** Transfer the peas and salmon to a blender and add enough of the steam water to cover halfway. Blend for 1 minute until the mixture forms a lumpy puree. Serve warm, reheating if necessary.

# sardines & sweet potato

Sardines really are the best type of fish, so get your baby loving them from a young age. Mixing them with sweet potato will make it easy. Cassie was a big fan of this dish from the very beginning.

**MAKES:**
4 servings

**PREPARATION TIME:**
10 minutes

**COOKING TIME:**
20 minutes

**STORAGE:**
Refrigerate for up to 2 days or freeze cubes of the cooled purée for up to 1 month.

1 sweet potato, unpeeled, chopped into 2.5cm/1in cubes
4 tinned sardines in oil or water, drained

1 Put the sweet potato in a steamer and steam, covered, over boiling water for 20 minutes until completely soft. Remove from the heat, transfer to a bowl and mash, using a fork.

2 In another bowl, mash the sardines and their bones well with a fork, then stir them into the sweet potato. Serve warm.

*sardines* are high in omega-3 fatty acids and protein. They're also a good source of vitamin D and calcium, which work together to promote stronger bones. They're a wonderful fast food, too.

# mackerel & broccoli

Your baby will love the rich texture of nutrient-rich mackerel. Serve this as suggested or mix it with a grain to add some complex carbohydrates.

**MAKES:**
4 servings

**PREPARATION TIME:**
5 minutes

**COOKING TIME:**
10 minutes

**STORAGE:**
Refrigerate for up to 2 days or freeze cubes of the cooled purée for up to 1 month.

115g/4oz broccoli, cut into 2.5cm/1in florets
85g/3oz smoked mackerel, deboned

1 Put the broccoli in a steamer and steam, covered, over boiling water for 10 minutes, or until completely soft. Reserve the steam water. If using a blender with a plastic container, leave to cool completely before blending.

2 Meanwhile, remove and discard the skin from the mackerel and remove any bones, feeling the flesh with your fingers. Shred the mackerel into a small bowl with a fork.

3 Transfer the broccoli to a blender and add enough of the steam water to cover halfway. Add the mackerel and blend for 1 minute until smooth, adding more steam water if necessary. Serve warm, reheating if necessary.

*mackerel* is packed with omega-3 fatty acids, selenium, and vitamins B6 and B12. Eating oily fish helps in the development of nerves and brain tissue. Avoid King Mackerel, though, which can have high mercury levels.

# beef & cauliflower

Organic beef is more expensive than conventional because it is a much higher-quality product. It's better to eat beef less frequently and eat it organically than to eat cheap conventional meat more often.

MAKES:
4 servings

PREPARATION TIME:
5 minutes

COOKING TIME:
15 minutes

STORAGE:
Refrigerate for up to 2 days or freeze cubes of the cooled purée for up to 1 month.

40g/1½oz cauliflower, cut into 2.5cm/1in florets
1 tsp olive oil
100g/3½oz lean beef mince

1 Put the cauliflower in a steamer and steam, covered, over boiling water for 15 minutes until completely soft. Reserve the steam water. Meanwhile, heat a small frying pan over a medium heat. Add the olive oil and when it is hot, add the mince. Cook for 10 minutes, stirring occasionally, until thoroughly cooked through. If using a blender with a plastic container, leave both the beef and cauliflower to cool completely before blending.

2 Transfer the beef and cauliflower to a blender. Blend for 1 minute, slowly adding a little of the steam water 1 tablespoon at a time, until smooth. Serve warm, reheating if necessary.

*beef* that is organic and grass-fed is low in fat and a great source of B vitamins. It's also rich in zinc, which is essential for normal growth, the immune system and appetite control.

# venison & parsnip

Wild meats offer another healthy alternative to intensively farmed meats. Venison's strong, earthy flavour is nicely balanced here by the parsnip.

MAKES:
4 servings

PREPARATION TIME:
5 minutes

COOKING TIME:
15 minutes

STORAGE:
Refrigerate for up to 2 days or freeze cubes of the cooled purée for up to 1 month.

40g/1½oz parsnip, cut into 5mm/¼in slices
2 tsp olive oil
100g/3½oz venison

1 Put the parsnip in a steamer and steam, covered, over boiling water for 15 minutes until completely soft. Reserve the steam water.

2 Meanwhile, heat a small frying pan over a medium heat. Add the olive oil and when it is hot, add the venison. Cook, partially covered, for 5 minutes until beginning to brown. Turn it over and cook, partially covered, for a further 5 minutes until thoroughly cooked through. If using a blender with a plastic container, leave both the venison and parsnip to cool completely before blending.

3 Transfer the venison and parsnip to a blender. Blend for 1 minute, slowly adding a little of the steam water 1 tablespoon at a time, until smooth. Serve warm, reheating if necessary.

# ▼ chicken & courgette

This delicious dish is sure to be a hit. Use organic chicken, especially for a baby. It is superior in quality, texture and taste and won't contain antibiotic residues.

MAKES:
4 servings

PREPARATION TIME:
5 minutes

COOKING TIME:
10 minutes

STORAGE:
Refrigerate for up to 2 days or freeze cubes of the cooled purée for up to 1 month.

2 tsp olive oil
1 boneless, skinless chicken breast, about 100g/3½oz, coarsely chopped
½ courgette, quartered lengthways and cut into 5mm/¼in-thick pieces

**1** Heat a small frying pan over a medium heat. Add the olive oil and when it is hot, add the chicken and courgette. Cook, covered, for 10 minutes, stirring occasionally, until the courgette is soft and the chicken is cooked through and the juices run clear. If using a blender with a plastic container, leave the mixture to cool completely before blending.

**2** Transfer the chicken and courgette to a blender and blend for 1–2 minutes until slightly chunky, or longer for a smoother consistency, adding a little water if necessary. Serve warm, reheating if necessary.

# Lumps to solids

Your baby's appetite is really growing! She's now getting the majority of her calories from food rather than breast milk or formula, so it's more important than ever to optimize her nutrition. Seeded fruits, such as kiwi and raspberries, are a great addition to her diet. Live natural yogurt is no longer just for soaking – she can eat it now on its own or mixed into her food. At this age, she's certainly ready to put her new teeth to use on more textured foods, too. This means that you can gradually start phasing out the purées and giving her little bits of food instead. Remember that variety is key in helping your baby to develop a love of good food. Buttery Grits, colourful Saucy Steam-Fry and flavourful Grilled Onion Chicken are just some of the delicious new options she's now ready to devour.

*Swede & Pak Choi (see page 65)*

# g to 12 months

The amount of food your baby is eating now can be quite impressive. Feel free to continue mixing and matching your frozen food cubes from chapters 1 and 2 in addition to trying the new recipes in this section. A good ratio to follow at this age is one part starch to one part vegetable, plus good seed oil and some protein. Add extra nutrition to your child's meals wherever you can. For example, sprinkle her beans and grains with finely chopped herbs, such as parsley or basil.

**FATS:** Good fats continue to be important, so keep giving your child two teaspoons of cold-pressed seed oil once each day. Carry on with other nutritious sources of essential fats as well, such as avocado and oily fish.

**YOGURT & KEFIR:** Carry on with breast milk or formula. I have always let my babies take as much breast milk as they like because it is such an excellent food, and by this stage they are naturally taking less. I offer it away from solid food, though, so it doesn't fill them up before they eat. If you're using formula, follow the instructions on the packet to determine how much to give your baby at this age. You can also introduce live, organic natural yogurt and kefir – both are good sources of calcium and protein, and they contain important probiotic bacteria that support good digestive health. Your baby's digestive system is still developing, though, so I recommend waiting a few more months before introducing other dairy products (see page 90).

**TEXTURE IN FOOD:** At this age, most children will be able to handle more texture in their food. You may be able to stop puréeing meals altogether, or you may have to purée them only a little. If she wasn't interested in finely grated or small pieces of raw fruits and vegetables before, she should be able to eat them now. As your baby's motor skills develop, finger foods will become more interesting to her, and she might be able to manage some pieces of peach, grapes or cucumber, peeled and deseeded. Cut fruit or vegetables into 5mm/¼in pieces to avoid choking and always sit with your child while she eats in case she needs your help. You can also add in fruit with little seeds now, such as kiwi and blackberries. Don't worry if your baby isn't chewing much yet and still needs a lot of things puréed. She'll get there soon.

**OATS:** Even though I don't introduce other grains that contain gluten until one year, I do introduce oats at nine months. They are a low-gluten grain, which makes them a good first choice to see how your child will handle the proteins in gluten. Use oats sparingly at first as she approaches one year. Unsalted rice cakes are still great when she's teething, but you could try introducing unsalted oatcakes as well (be careful of choking). Or try the Berry

& Oat Porridge on page 58 for breakfast. Watch for any reaction in your baby. If she does react, wait eight weeks and then try again.

**SPROUTS:** You can introduce sprouts now, too. Sprouts are considered 'live foods' because the seeds are germinating and growing. The nutrition in live foods is far superior to other foods. The living enzymes in the sprouts aid our digestion and our assimilation of nutrients. This also makes them very easy to digest. Toss them in the blender when you purée your baby's meal or chop them and mix them into her food. You really can't overuse them, and you're adding a phenomenal course of nutrition.

## NEW FOODS TO INTRODUCE AT 9–12 MONTHS

*Your child is now ready for the foods listed in the chart below. Combine them with the foods listed in the previous chapters to give her the best variety you can.*

| FRUITS | VEGETABLES | GRAINS | FISH* | DAIRY & EGGS | FATS |
|---|---|---|---|---|---|
| • blackberry<br>• blueberry<br>• cranberry (fresh or unsweetened dried)<br>• currant<br>• date<br>• fig<br>• grape<br>• kiwi<br>• lychee<br>• raisin<br>• raspberry<br>• rhubarb | • asparagus<br>• Chinese leaf<br>• cucumber<br>• fennel<br>• garlic<br>• fresh herbs, such as basil, mint and parsley<br>• Jerusalem artichoke<br>• onion<br>• pak choi<br>• spring onion<br>• sprouts (all types, including alfalfa, broccoli, chickpea and lentil) | • corn<br>• oat | * Avoid overfished varieties, such as cod<br><br>• haddock<br>• pollock<br>• trout | • kefir<br>• yogurt | • butter |

With my kids, I found that I had a feeding window. If I didn't get all the food in their mouths within twenty minutes – thirty minutes tops – they would lose interest or the little bit of food they had eaten would hit their stomach and make them feel full. So try to get the meal in as quickly as is comfortable. I also found that my kids got restless after a short while, so I always had little toys on the table to keep them busy at this age. If they're happy at the table, you can keep putting food in their mouths. When the kids are older and feeding themselves, I don't allow toys, but at this age they can be a huge help.

EATING ON THE GO: You'll be out and about a lot now, and taking snacks or food with you is easy. A little pot of cut-up fruit or a banana is a great portable snack that your baby can eat in her buggy or in a high chair when you go out. It'll keep her busy and give you a chance to relax with a friend over a cup of coffee. Many of the meals in this and the previous chapters are portable, too. Fish and meat dishes require refrigeration, though, so save them for meals at home. Instead, take a pot of grain mixed with bean or vegetables if you're out for a couple of hours. Just remember to bring a bib, spoon, bottle of filtered water and some paper towels or wipes.

## Meals for Yourself

You're doing a lot of cooking for your baby right now. You may be buying lots of new ingredients that you haven't traditionally used, and your fridge might be full of food with which you're not that familiar. Remember that these foods aren't just for children. You can do a lot to boost your own energy and overall sense of well-being right now by making sure you eat just as healthily as your baby. Instead of letting things spoil and get tossed into the bin, make a quick supper for yourself and your partner. If you're tired at the end of the day and have no idea what the two of you should eat, cook some pasta, steam some of the veggies you've got, throw on some seeds, drizzle with olive oil – and relax. It doesn't need to be a big production to be satisfying, nutritious and delicious.

## Avoiding Waste

Now that your fridge is full of great new ingredients, try to use things quickly so they don't spoil. It's a shame to throw away good food just because you forgot about it or didn't have time to cook. One way to avoid this is to make sure you're storing foods properly. Each recipe in this book includes storage instructions that will let you know if a food is suitable to be frozen or refrigerated.

Remember that air makes food stale, so put leftover foods and things like crackers, grains, biscuits and rice cakes in airtight containers so that they will stay fresh longer.

## MEAL PLANNER FOR BABIES AT 9–12 MONTHS

*This meal planner uses all the recipes in this chapter over the course of a week.*
*Even if you make only the majority, you and your baby will be doing really well.*

| DAY | BREAKFAST | MID-MORNING | LUNCH | MID-AFTERNOON | TEA | EVENING |
|---|---|---|---|---|---|---|
| 1 | Gluten-Free Porridge with Dates (see page 59) with 2 tsp seed oil | breast/bottle | Brown Rice & Sprouts (see page 65) sweet potato (see Carrot Purée on page 29) warm water | breast/bottle | Pollock with Green Beans (see page 68) with 2 tsp olive oil warm water | breast/bottle |
| 2 | rice puffs with yogurt | breast/bottle | Jerusalem Artichoke & Onion Simmer (see page 64) Carrot Purée (see page 29) warm water | breast/bottle | Swede & Pak Choi (see page 65) Quinoa Purée (see page 33) with 2 tsp seed oil warm water | breast/bottle |
| 3 | Berry & Oat Porridge (see page 58) with 2 tsp seed oil | breast/bottle | Cannellini Beans & Amaranth (see page 64) Butternut Squash Purée (see page 30) warm water | breast/bottle | Grilled Onion Chicken (see page 67) with 2 tsp olive oil Broccoli & Cauliflower Purée (see page 29) warm water | breast/bottle |
| 4 | cornflakes (no added sugar) with rice milk | breast/bottle | Buttered Turnip Sauté (see page 61) beetroot purée (see Butternut Squash Purée page 30) with 2 tsp olive oil warm water | breast/bottle | Quinoa, Chinese Leaves & Carrot Stew (see page 61) 2 tsp seed oil warm water | breast/bottle |
| 5 | Fruit Ambrosia (see page 60) unsalted oatcakes | breast/bottle | Saucy Steam-Fry (see page 62) Amaranth Purée (see page 32) with 2 tsp seed oil warm water | breast/bottle | Beef & Cauliflower (see page 50) with 2 tsp olive oil Mangetout, Cucumber & Yogurt Salad (see page 67) warm water | breast/bottle |
| 6 | Millet Purée (see page 33) mango (see Apple Purée on page 26) | breast/bottle | Avocado Mash (see page 28) with millet flakes and yogurt warm water | breast/bottle | Baby Brown Rice Purée (see page 30) pumpkin (see Butternut Squash Purée on page 30) with 2 tsp seed oil warm water | breast/bottle |
| 7 | Grits (see page 59) | breast/bottle | Red Lentil Purée (see page 34) Quinoa Purée (see page 33) steamed carrot warm water | breast/bottle | Sardines & Sweet Potato (see page 49) grated raw swede warm water | breast/bottle |

# ▲ berry & oat porridge

Soaked porridge is a family favourite – and incredibly versatile. The sweet, tart berries featured in this version will be a great flavour experience for your baby, but you can use any mixture of stewed or fresh fruits. (From 15 months you can add ground seeds and/or nuts, too.)

**MAKES:**
4 servings

**PREPARATION TIME:**
5 minutes, plus overnight soaking

**COOKING TIME:**
10 minutes

**STORAGE:**
Refrigerate for up to 3 days or freeze for up to 3 months.

**115g/4oz/1 heaped cup porridge oats**
**1 tbsp kefir or natural yogurt**
**250ml/9fl oz/1 cup natural yogurt**
**125g/4½oz/1 cup berries, such as raspberries, blueberries or blackberries**

**1** Put the oats and kefir in a small saucepan. Add 750ml/26fl oz/3 cups water and leave to soak, covered, overnight at room temperature.

**2** Bring the soaked oats to a simmer over a medium heat, then reduce the heat to low and cook, stirring occasionally, for 10 minutes until soft and creamy. Remove from the heat.

**3** Mix in the yogurt and berries. If the mixture is too coarse, transfer it to a blender and blend for 1 minute until smooth. If using a blender with a plastic container, leave the porridge to cool completely before blending. Serve warm, reheating if necessary.

# gluten-free porridge with dates

MAKES:
4 servings

PREPARATION
TIME:
5 minutes

COOKING TIME:
15 minutes

STORAGE:
Refrigerate for
up to 3 days or
freeze for up to
3 months.

This easy and delicious porridge uses three gluten-free grains. It's one of my favourite creations, and Jessie, Nicholas and Cassie love it.

3 tbsp millet flakes
3 tbsp quinoa flakes
3 tbsp buckwheat flakes
3 tbsp chopped dried
   dates

**1** Put all of the ingredients and 455ml/16fl oz/scant 2 cups water in a medium saucepan. Bring to a simmer over a medium heat, then reduce the heat to low and cook for 15 minutes, stirring continuously, until soft. Remove from the heat and leave to cool a little. Serve warm.

**2** If a smoother consistency is desired, transfer the mixture to a blender (leaving it to cool completely first if using a blender with a plastic container) and blend for 1 minute until smooth. Serve warm, reheating if necessary.

# grits

SERVES:
2 adults and
2 children

PREPARATION
TIME:
5 minutes

COOKING TIME:
20 minutes

STORAGE:
Not suitable
for storage.

Grits are a traditional corn dish from the American South. This gorgeous, buttery dish makes a fabulous breakfast that the entire family can enjoy. You can also serve it as a side dish – in the southern United States, it's often eaten with pork. (Once your baby has reached one year, you can add ¾ teaspoon salt in step 1.)

225g/8oz/1½ cups
   coarsely ground
   polenta (hominy grits)
175g/6oz butter, cut into
   6 pieces

**1** In a medium saucepan, bring 1.4l/48fl oz/5½ cups water to the boil. Add the polenta and whisk quickly with a wire whisk until the mixture is smooth and has no lumps. Reduce the heat to medium-low and simmer very gently for 20 minutes until thick, stirring with the whisk every few minutes.

**2** Remove from the heat and divide into four bowls. Top each child portion with 1 piece of the butter and each adult portion with 2 pieces. Serve hot.

*polenta*
is great for a healthy heart. It contains lots of folate, a B vitamin that helps lower levels of homocysteine, an amino acid that can be dangerous at high levels.

# ▼ fruit ambrosia

MAKES:
2 servings

PREPARATION
TIME:
10 minutes

STORAGE:
Refrigerate for
up to 1 day.

You could serve this versatile recipe with cooked grains instead of millet flakes if you prefer. It makes a fabulous base for smoothies, too: just omit the millet flakes and add any other fruits from this or previous chapters to create a great mid-morning or mid-afternoon drink snack.

**1 banana, peeled**
**55g/2oz seedless red**
**grapes**
**1 kiwi, peeled and**
**roughly chopped**
**4 tbsp Greek yogurt**
**4 tbsp instant millet**
**flakes**

**1** Put the banana, grapes, kiwi and yogurt in a blender and pulse a few times until lumpy.

**2** Divide the mixture into two bowls, then stir 2 tablespoons of the millet flakes into each portion and serve.

*yogurt*
is a health-promoting wonderfood that gives your baby good bacteria, protein, calcium, vitamin B12 and other nutrients. Offer it plain or mixed with cereals, nuts and fruits.

# buttered turnip sauté

Your little one won't be able to get enough of these succulent, buttery turnips. A versatile, often overlooked vegetable, turnips are great raw, too. Try serving them finely grated into salads.

**MAKES:**
4 servings

**PREPARATION TIME:**
10 minutes

**COOKING TIME:**
10 minutes

**STORAGE:**
Refrigerate for up to 3 days or freeze cubes of the mash for up to 3 months.

30g/1oz butter
200g/7oz turnips, quartered and cut into 5mm/¼in-thick slices

**1** Melt the butter in a large frying pan over a low heat. Add the turnips and cook for 10 minutes until completely soft. Stir occasionally to ensure they cook evenly.

**2** Mash the turnips, using a fork, and serve warm. If a smoother consistency is desired, transfer to a blender (leaving it to cool completely first if using a blender with a plastic container) and blend for 1 minute until smooth. Serve warm, reheating if necessary.

# quinoa, chinese leaves & carrot stew

This colourful stew makes a quick, delicious meal. Chinese leaves are great – they can also be used finely chopped in salads and on sandwiches.

**MAKES:**
4 servings

**PREPARATION TIME:**
10 minutes

**COOKING TIME:**
35 minutes

**STORAGE:**
Refrigerate for up to 3 days or freeze cubes of the stew for up to 3 months.

55g/2oz/⅓ cup quinoa
1 carrot, cut into 1cm/½in-thick rounds
2 heads of Chinese leaves, about 115g/4oz, cut into 1cm/½in squares

**1** Put the quinoa in a sieve and rinse under cold running water, then drain well. Transfer to a medium saucepan and toast over a high heat for 5 minutes, stirring continuously, until any excess water has evaporated and the quinoa has browned slightly and begun to pop.

**2** Slowly add 455ml/16fl oz/scant 2 cups water and bring to the boil over a high heat. Reduce the heat to low and simmer, covered, for 10 minutes. Add the carrots and simmer, covered, for a further 10 minutes, then add the Chinese leaves. Continue simmering, covered, for a further 10 minutes until the grain and vegetables are very soft. If using a blender with a plastic container, leave the mixture to cool completely before blending.

**3** Transfer the mixture to a blender. Blend for 1 minute or until the desired consistency is achieved. Serve warm, reheating if necessary.

*quinoa* is a complete protein This means it contains all the essential amino acids your child needs, including cystine, lysine and methionine – amino acids that are low in other grains.

# saucy steam-fry

MAKES:
4 servings

PREPARATION
TIME:
15 minutes

COOKING TIME:
20 minutes

STORAGE:
Refrigerate for
up to 3 days.

The visual impact of food is important for children. They love bright colours, and this dish is bursting with them. The orange, white and green vegetables cut into pretty little shapes are sure to catch your baby's eye and get her excited about this meal.

2 tsp kuzu
1 tbsp toasted sesame oil
1 carrot, quartered
    lengthways and cut
    into 5mm/¼in-thick
    discs
55g/2oz cauliflower, cut
    into 1cm/½in florets
40g/1½oz broccoli, cut
    into 1cm/½in florets
1 tsp mirin
55g/2oz/1 cup dried corn
    pasta
salt

**1** In a small bowl, mix together the kuzu and 1 tablespoon cold water, stirring until the kuzu has dissolved, then set aside.

**2** Heat a wok or large frying pan over a medium-low heat. Add the sesame oil, carrot and 4 tablespoons hot water. Steam-fry, stirring frequently, for 5 minutes. As the pan begins to dry out, add another 4 tablespoons hot water. Cook for a further 5 minutes until the carrot has begun to soften. Meanwhile, bring a large pan of salted water to the boil and cook the pasta for 2 minutes longer than the packet instructions so it is very soft, then drain.

**3** Add the cauliflower and another 4 tablespoons hot water to the wok and steam-fry for a further 3 minutes, stirring frequently, until the cauliflower has begun to soften. Add the broccoli and another 60ml/2fl oz/¼ cup hot water and continue steam-frying, stirring occasionally, for a further 5 minutes.

**4** Stir the kuzu mixture and mirin into the vegetables and cook, stirring, for a further 2 minutes until the vegetables are tender and the sauce is thick and shimmery. Remove from the heat.

**5** Divide the pasta into four bowls and top each portion with one-quarter of the steam-fry. Serve warm. If a smoother consistency is desired, transfer the pasta and vegetables to a blender (leaving them to cool completely first if using a blender with a plastic container) and pulse a few times until lumpy. If using a blender with a plastic container, leave the pasta and vegetables to cool completely before blending. Serve warm, reheating if necessary.

*kuzu*
is an outstanding
gelling and thickening
agent that also has soothing
medicinal effects. It can relieve
digestive problems, and its
high flavanoid content aids
circulation by helping
to dilate blood
vessels.

# cannellini beans & amaranth

Combining creamy cannellini beans with subtly sweet amaranth makes a delicious protein meal.

**MAKES:**
4 servings

**PREPARATION TIME:**
5 minutes, plus overnight soaking and making the amaranth purée

**COOKING TIME:**
1 hour 40 minutes

**STORAGE:**
Refrigerate for up to 3 days or freeze cubes of the purée for up to 3 months.

85g/3oz/½ cup dried cannellini beans
2 tsp lemon juice
1 strip of kombu, about 8 x 5cm/3¼ x 2in, cut into little pieces
4 portions Amaranth Purée (see page 34)

**1** Put the beans and lemon juice in a medium saucepan, cover with water and leave to soak, covered, overnight.

**2** Drain and rinse the beans. Return them to the pan and add 570ml/20fl oz/scant 2⅓ cups water. Bring to the boil over a high heat and boil for 10 minutes, skimming any scum that rises to the surface. Reduce the heat to low, add the kombu and cook, covered, for 1½ hours until the beans are completely soft, then discard the kombu.

**3** Mash with a fork, then mix with an equal portion of the amaranth purée and serve warm. If a smoother consistency is desired, transfer the mixture to a blender (leaving it to cool completely first if using a blender with a plastic container) and pulse for 1 minute or until the desired consistency is achieved. Serve warm, reheating if necessary.

# jerusalem artichoke & onion simmer

Jerusalem artichokes are a bit like potatoes with a hint of artichoke flavour. The hotter the raw onion, the sweeter it is when cooked, so if you're crying while you're chopping, your kids will probably love it.

**MAKES:**
8 servings

**PREPARATION TIME:**
10 minutes

**COOKING TIME:**
30 minutes

**STORAGE:**
Refrigerate for up to 3 days or freeze cubes of the mixture for up to 3 months.

1 tbsp olive oil
350g/12oz Jerusalem artichokes, trimmed and sliced into disks
1 small onion, finely chopped

**1** Heat a large saucepan over a medium-low heat and add the oil. When it is hot, add the artichokes, onion and enough water to just cover the vegetables. Simmer, covered, for 30 minutes, stirring occasionally and adding a little water if the mixture starts to dry out.

**2** Mash with a fork and serve warm. If a smoother consistency is desired, transfer the mixture to a blender (leaving it to cool completely first if using a blender with a plastic container) and blend for 1 minute or until the desired consistency is achieved. Serve warm, reheating if necessary.

# swede & pak choi

A beautiful dish, the green pak choi creates visual appeal, while its clean, fresh flavour brightens up the more sombre swede.

**MAKES:**
4 servings

**PREPARATION TIME:**
10 minutes

**COOKING TIME:**
25 minutes

**STORAGE:**
Refrigerate for up to 3 days or freeze cubes of the mixture for up to 3 months.

450g/1lb swede, peeled and cut into 1cm/½in cubes
70g/2½oz pak choi, cut into 1cm/½in-wide strips

**1** Put the swede in a steamer and steam, covered, over boiling water for 20 minutes until completely soft, then remove from the steamer and set aside. Reserve the steam water.

**2** Put the pak choi in the steamer and steam, covered, over boiling water for 3 minutes until wilted. Reserve the steam water. If using a blender with a plastic container, leave the vegetables to cool completely before blending.

**3** Transfer the vegetables to the blender and pulse for 1 minute until the mixture forms a lumpy purée, slowly adding a little of the steam water if necessary. If a smoother consistency is desired, blend for a little longer. Serve warm, reheating if necessary.

# brown rice & sprouts

One of Nicholas's favourites, this dish is brilliant on its own or as a base into which you can mix other foods. Using sprouted seeds is a lovely way to add vitality to your growing child's diet.

**MAKES:**
4 servings

**PREPARATION TIME:**
5 minutes, plus at least 7 hours soaking

**COOKING TIME:**
1 hour

**STORAGE:**
Refrigerate for up to 2 days or freeze cubes of the mixture for up to 1 month. Reheat until hot.

100g/3½oz/½ cup short grain brown rice
1 tbsp kefir or natural yogurt
1 garlic clove, crushed
55g/2oz alfalfa sprouts

**1** Put the rice, kefir and 570ml/20fl oz/scant 2⅓ cups warm water in a medium saucepan and leave to soak, covered, for 7 hours or overnight.

**2** Add the garlic to the rice and bring to the boil over a high heat, then reduce the heat to low and simmer, covered, for 1 hour until the rice is very tender. If using a blender with a plastic container, leave the mixture to cool completely before blending.

**3** Transfer the mixture to a blender, add the sprouts and blend for 1 minute until smooth. Serve warm, reheating if necessary.

*sprouts* are one of the most complex, nutritional foods. They're rich in vitamins, minerals and proteins. What really sets these 'live foods' apart are their enzymes, which boost the digestive system.

# ◄ mangetout, cucumber & yogurt salad

**MAKES:**
1 serving

**PREPARATION TIME:**
10 minutes

**COOKING TIME:**
10 minutes

**STORAGE:**
Not suitable for storage.

Fresh vegetables mixed with yogurt make a delicious first salad for your little one – and this combination was a big hit with Jessie. For variation, add chopped cucumber and avocado. (From one year, you can add chopped tomato, too.)

4 mangetout, cut into bite-sized pieces
40g/1½oz cucumber, peeled, deseeded and cut into bite-sized pieces
1 tsp natural yogurt

1 Put the mangetout in a steamer and steam, covered, over boiling water for 10 minutes until soft. Remove from the heat and leave to cool completely.

2 Put the mangetout, cucumber and yogurt in a small bowl, mix well and serve. If a smoother consistency is desired, transfer the mixture to a blender and pulse a few times until the desired consistency is achieved, then serve.

# grilled onion chicken

**MAKES:**
2 servings

**PREPARATION TIME:**
5 minutes

**COOKING TIME:**
11 minutes

**STORAGE:**
Refrigerate for up to 2 days or freeze cubes of the mixture for up to 1 month.

Grilling brings out great flavours in the onion and the chicken. Use organic chicken and you get meat with less water and more flavour.

1 tsp olive oil
55g/2oz boneless, skinless chicken breast, cut into small chunks
1 small onion, finely chopped

1 Preheat the grill to medium and grease a medium, shallow baking tin with the oil. Put the chicken and onion in the baking dish and grill for 6–7 minutes until the onion and chicken begin to brown.

2 Remove from the grill, stir and then grill for a further 3–4 minutes until the chicken is cooked through and the juices run clear. Serve warm.

3 If a smoother consistency is desired, transfer the chicken and onion to a blender (leaving it to cool completely first if using a blender with a plastic container). Pulse for 1 minute, or until the desired consistency is achieved, then serve warm, reheating if necessary.

# pollock with green beans

Pollock is mild, lean, tender fish. The fillets are usually bone-free with a consistent snow-white colour. It flakes easily, making it perfect for kids – and it's a great alternative to overfished cod.

**MAKES:**
4 servings

**PREPARATION TIME:**
10 minutes

**COOKING TIME:**
15 minutes

**STORAGE:**
Refrigerate the fish for up to 2 days or freeze in cubes for up to 1 month. Refrigerate the beans for up to 3 days or freeze in cubes for up to 3 months.

**100g/3½oz green beans, trimmed and cut into 2.5cm/1in-long pieces**
**1½ tsp olive oil**
**100g/3½oz pollock fillet, rinsed**

**1** Put the green beans in a steamer and steam, covered, over boiling water for 15 minutes until completely soft.

**2** While the beans are steaming, heat a small frying pan over a medium heat. Add ½ teaspoon of the olive oil and when it is hot, add the pollock, skin-side up. Cook, covered, for 5 minutes, then turn the fish over and cook, covered, for a further 5–10 minutes until white. Remove from the heat, then remove and discard the skin.

**3** Cut the fish roughly, checking with your fingers for bones, then transfer to a bowl and mash with a fork. If a smoother consistency is desired, transfer the fish to a blender and blend for 1 minute until smooth. If using a blender with a plastic container, leave the fish and beans to cool completely before blending.

**4** Transfer the beans to a clean blender, add the remaining olive oil and pulse for 1 minute until the mixture forms a lumpy purée. Serve warm with the fish, reheating if necessary.

*white fish*
is the best source of low-fat animal protein. Protein is vital for a strong immune system and the development of healthy bones, skin, nails and hair. Packed with vitamins and minerals, white fish also provides metabolism-boosting iodine and B vitamins.

# eating more

Between his first birthday and the time he turns two, your baby will reach some remarkable developmental milestones. If he hasn't already taken his first steps, he will very soon. Before you know it, he'll be off and running – with you in quick pursuit. In the coming months, he'll start talking and acquiring lots of new motor skills as well. All of this growth and energy requires fuel, and the best fuel you can continue to give him is a nutrition-packed diet. He's now ready for some great new foods, such as potatoes, tomatoes, eggs and whole grains like barley, rye and spelt. From 15 months, he can also have seeds, nuts and wheat. With delicious options like Spelt French Toast, Best Beef Burgers, Quesadillas and Tuna Pie, mealtimes are about to become significantly more exciting.

*Quesadillas (see page 101)*

# 12 to 15 months

With such a huge variety of foods and ingredients in your baby's diet now, it's easy to provide him with a wonderful mix of tastes, textures and nutrients. Whether or not you continue breastfeeding is a very personal decision and will be influenced by many factors. If you can or want to, carry on with breast milk or formula. Your baby will naturally take much less milk now because the majority of his nutrition is coming from food. By one year, my babies and I had settled into a comfortable feeding schedule. I found that there were two times in the day, once in the morning and once at night, when I liked to breastfeed. As a working mother, this made sense for me, but if you find that a different schedule suits you better, go with that.

**WEANING OFF BREAST MILK:** If you wean your baby off breast milk or formula now, I don't recommend replacing it with cow's milk (see page 13). You can rely on yogurt and a wide variety of foods for calcium and magnesium, or you can offer organic goat's or sheep's milk if you really want to. If you do use cow's milk, buy organic milk – it not only excludes hormone residues and antibiotic residues, it also offers more nutrition.

**CHEWING:** If your baby is still not chewing a lot, simply continue with mushy or lumpy purées for now to ensure that he is getting a good quantity of food, and continue encouraging him with finger foods like rice cakes and small pieces of raw fruit and vegetables. You may find that some of the recipes in this section, such as Fried Egg on Rye and Best Beef Burgers, will have to wait until he has mastered the art of chewing. If that's the case, just try some of the softer foods, such as Cornbread Pudding and Mashed Potato Craters, and continue with the recipes from the previous chapters. The rest can wait until later. Again, there is no rush. And if there's any doubt, it's better to go with softer food anyway so that you know he's properly digesting and assimilating what he eats.

**EGGS:** You can offer eggs now, which are an excellent source of protein. Some people worry about salmonella, but I don't get overly worried about foods being dangerous. After three kids and lots and lots of eggs, I have never had a problem. Just make sure you buy organic eggs, which are produced in less-crowded conditions where disease does not spread as easily as in conventional farming. I don't like to overcook eggs, but for this age, I tend to scramble or fry them with the yolk broken so that I can see that they are cooked.

**SOYA:** You can also offer soya from one year old, but I recommend keeping it to a minimum for both children and adults. Soya contains phytoestrogens, which may disrupt the body's hormone balance. As I mentioned earlier, in countries where soya and its products are traditionally eaten, they are consumed only in small amounts and not as a protein substitute. Tofu is fine once in a while, but tempeh is better because it is fermented, contains valuable B vitamins and is easier to digest.

NIGHTSHADES: Your baby is now ready to eat aubergines, potatoes and tomatoes. Although these are very common foods, I wait to introduce them until after one year because they belong to the nightshade family of vegetables. This means that they contain a particular group of substances, called alkaloids, which can impact on nerve-muscle function and digestive function, and may also compromise joint function. These foods

## NEW FOODS TO INTRODUCE AT 12–15 MONTHS

*Your child is now ready for the foods listed in the chart below. Combine them with the foods listed in the previous chapters to give him the best variety you can.*

| FRUITS | VEGETABLES | GRAINS | PULSES | DAIRY & EGGS |
|---|---|---|---|---|
| • citrus (in small amounts): clementine kumquat lemon lime mandarin pomelo satsuma tangelo tangerine<br><br>No orange or grapefruit<br><br>• passion fruit<br>• pomegranate<br>• strawberry | • aubergine<br>• cabbage<br>• caper<br>• chard<br>• gherkin<br>• green pepper<br>• kale<br>• lettuce<br>• mushroom<br>• olives (pitted)<br>• potato<br>• rocket<br>• spinach<br>• sweetcorn<br>• sweet pepper (red, yellow, orange, etc)<br>• tomato<br>• watercress | • barley<br>• Kamut<br>• rye<br>• spelt | • soya (keep to a minimum), including tempeh and tofu | • eggs |

do have nutritional benefits; it's just a good idea not to become too dependent on them. As you know by now, there are so many other foods to enjoy.

**SPINACH:** Spinach is an easy vegetable to overuse, and it can sometimes be difficult to digest, so I wait until one year to introduce it. By then, your baby's digestive system is mature enough to handle it.

**MUSHROOMS:** I also wait until one year to introduce mushrooms. Although they're very nutritious, they contain a high percentage of chitin, a polysaccharide that is difficult to digest. Cooking is essential to break down the chitinous cell walls. As with other foods in earlier chapters, if your child gets an upset tummy or other reaction after eating them, give him a bit more time and try again in six to eight weeks.

**SOUPS:** When your child is very young and first adjusting to food, it's important that he doesn't fill up with watery meals. Now that he's eating more solid food and getting much less breast milk or formula (if any), you can introduce soups. They're a good way to incorporate grains, pulses and vegetables into his diet. The soups in this chapter are substantial enough to make a meal, especially when served with some kind of protein.

**GLUTEN:** At one year, your baby's digestive system should be mature enough to handle most gluten, so you can begin to offer pastas. Look for wholemeal spelt or Kamut pasta and alternate them with gluten-free alternatives, such as buckwheat noodles and corn pasta. I suggest cooking pasta for a couple of minutes longer than recommended on the packet so it's soft, which will allow your baby to easily chew and digest it. If you've been eating white pasta and make the switch to wholemeal pastas when you introduce them to your baby, I think you'll be delighted with the lovely flavour and texture the wholemeal grains give this familiar food. Note, however, that although grains containing gluten are fine for a one-year-old child, I do not introduce wheat until fifteen months. This is because grains such as spelt are better nutritionally, and it's much too easy to consume too much wheat. Let your child experience these other grains first and get used to them before giving him wheat.

**BREADS & CRACKERS:** It's great to be able to offer your child bread and crackers made from spelt, Kamut, barley or rye. They make convenient, portable snacks and are a good carrier for spreads like hummus and seed butters. To relieve teething discomfort, you can give him grissini, crispbreads and crackers made from these grains, too.

Breads and crackers are easy to get a hold of, but make sure you don't give up all the great habits and other foods you have been using until now. Keep giving him different grains, such as brown rice, millet and quinoa – if he's chewing well, you won't even have to purée them any more. Raw vegetables, cut into sticks or disks, and fresh or dried fruit are still good for snacking. Make sure your baby continues to get a good range of foods with lots of variation in flavours, textures and colours.

# MEAL PLANNER FOR TODDLERS AT 12–15 MONTHS

*Don't be daunted by how many recipes there are on this meal planner. Follow it as closely as is comfortable, and make and freeze batches wherever possible.*

| DAY | BREAKFAST | MID-MORNING | LUNCH | MID-AFTERNOON | TEA |
|---|---|---|---|---|---|
| 1 | Mustard Scrambled Eggs (see page 78) rye toast | fruit (fresh or dried) | Tomato Soup with Rice (see page 81) with 2 tsp seed oil  nori squares | corn cakes | Chicken & Mushroom Pasta (see page 88)  raw peas |
| 2 | cornflakes (no added sugar) with yogurt | fruit (fresh or dried) | Fried Egg on Rye (see page 78)  celery sticks | oatcakes | Baked Beans with Jacket Potatoes (see page 83)  grated Cheddar cheese  steamed broccoli with 2 tsp seed oil |
| 3 | Wholemeal Spelt Pancakes (see page 76) | fruit (fresh or dried) | Millet Purée (see page 33)  sweet potato (see Carrot Purée on page 29) with 2 tsp olive oil | low-salt/baked tortillas | Best Beef Burgers (see page 88)  steamed carrot with 2 tsp seed oil |
| 4 | Cornbread Pudding (see page 79) | fruit (fresh or dried) | Squash & Potato Soup (see page 80) with 2 tsp olive oil  steamed mangetout | low-salt popcorn | Amaranth Purée (see page 32) with sprouts and 2 tsp seed oil  smoked salmon  sweet pepper |
| 5 | Spelt French Toast (see page 79) | fruit (fresh or dried) | Creamy Rustic Soup (see page 82) with 2 tsp seed oil | Japanese rice crackers | Grilled Cherry Tomato Spaghetti (see page 84)  steamed cauliflower |
| 6 | Gluten-Free Porridge with Dates (see page 59) with 2 tsp seed oil | fruit (fresh or dried) | Mashed Potato Craters (see page 84)  olives  steamed courgette | wholemeal grissini or pretzels | Wholegrain Risotto with Asparagus (see page 87)  grilled fish  grated beetroot with 2 tsp seed oil |
| 7 | seed- and nut-free muesli with rice milk | fruit (fresh or dried) | Pollock with Green Beans (see page 68) with 2 tsp olive oil  wholemeal spelt toast | wholemeal rye crackers/crispbreads | Saucy Steam-Fry (see page 62)  chopped rocket with 2 tsp seed oil |

# wholemeal spelt pancakes

Transform the relatively unhealthy breakfast of white-flour pancakes into a nutritious – and delicious – meal by using wholemeal spelt flour. Pancakes travel well and make a great snack for a hungry toddler.

**SERVES:**
2 adults and
2 children

**PREPARATION
TIME:**
10 minutes

**COOKING TIME:**
30 minutes

**STORAGE:**
Refrigerate the
uncooked batter
for up to 2 days.
Refrigerate the
cooked pancakes
for up to 3 days.

**325g/11½oz/2¾ cups
wholemeal spelt flour
1 tbsp baking powder
½ tsp salt
1 egg, beaten
350ml/12fl oz/scant
1½ cups rice milk,
plus extra as needed
2 tbsp olive oil, plus extra
for frying
70g/2½oz/½ cup
blueberries, chopped
strawberries or
chopped banana
(optional)**

**To serve:
butter
maple syrup
½ lemon, cut into wedges
sugar**

**1** Preheat the oven to 70°C/150°F/Gas ¼. In a small bowl, mix together the flour, baking powder and salt. In a medium bowl, whisk together the egg, rice milk and olive oil. Pour the dry mixture into the wet ingredients and whisk until smooth. Using a wooden spoon or rubber spatula, fold in the blueberries, if using.

**2** Heat a griddle over a medium-low heat until hot or heat a little olive oil in a large frying pan. For each pancake, drop 1–2 tablespoonfuls of the batter onto the hot griddle. The pancakes will spread to about 5cm/2in wide, so space them slightly apart. If the batter is too thick and the pancakes don't spread, add a little more rice milk 1 tablespoon at a time to thin out the batter. Cook for 2 minutes or until the bubbles that appear on the surface pop and the undersides of the pancakes are lightly browned.

**3** Flip the pancakes over. If they stick to the griddle, they are not ready to be turned; leave them to cook a little longer and then flip. Cook the other side of the pancakes for 1–2 minutes until lightly browned. Transfer to a plate and keep warm in the oven while you make the remaining pancakes. If using a frying pan, add more oil to the pan as necessary before each batch.

**4** Spread each pancake with a little butter and serve hot drizzled with maple syrup or sprinkled with lemon juice and sugar.

*spelt*
is an ancient grain
related to wheat.
It offers a broader
spectrum of nutrients than
hybridized wheat, and
people with sensitivities
to wheat can often eat
spelt instead.

# mustard scrambled eggs

SERVES:
2 adults and
2 children

PREPARATION
TIME:
5 minutes

COOKING TIME:
4 minutes

STORAGE:
Not suitable
for storage.

Protein-packed scrambled eggs are easy for small children to eat. Give your baby a spoon and he should be able to scoop them up from a bowl. The mustard gives them a flavour boost that will spark his interest.

**30g/1oz butter**
**8 eggs, beaten**
**¼ tsp salt**
**1 tbsp non-hot mustard**

**1** Melt the butter in a large frying pan over a medium-high heat until gently sizzling. Pour the eggs into the pan and sprinkle with the salt. Cook for 1 minute or until the edges of the eggs start to sizzle, then stir with a small wooden spoon for 2–3 minutes until just cooked. Remove from the heat.

**2** Stir in the mustard and serve immediately.

# fried egg on rye

SERVES:
2 adults and
2 children

PREPARATION
TIME:
5 minutes

COOKING TIME:
5 minutes

STORAGE:
Not suitable
for storage.

If your baby can chew, this is a good lunch. Nicholas loves how the egg gets a little crunchy when it's fried in the butter, and it's delicious with the toasted rye bread and mayonnaise.

**30g/1oz butter**
**6 eggs**
**mayonnaise, to taste,**
**for spreading**
**6 slices of wholemeal**
**rye bread**

**1** Melt the butter in a large frying pan over a medium-high heat. When it is sizzling hot, break the eggs into the pan one at a time and gently break the yolks. Work in batches if necessary.

**2** Reduce the heat to medium and cook for 5 minutes or until the eggs are just cooked. Meanwhile, toast the bread.

**3** Spread some mayonnaise on each slice of bread and top with 1 egg. Serve warm.

# spelt french toast

A great breakfast that combines carbs with protein – and a little sweetness. It's hard not to love this dish, no matter how old you are.

**SERVES:**
2 adults and
2 children

**PREPARATION TIME:**
5 minutes

**COOKING TIME:**
20 minutes

**STORAGE:**
Not suitable
for storage.

6 eggs, beaten
3 tbsp sugar
6 tbsp rice milk
¼ tsp vanilla extract
30g/1oz butter
6 slices of wholemeal
   spelt bread

**1** Preheat the oven to 70°C/150°F/Gas ¼. Put the eggs, sugar, rice milk and vanilla extract in a shallow bowl or baking dish and mix well until the sugar has dissolved.

**2** Melt the butter in a large frying pan over a medium heat until hot. Put 1 slice of bread in the baking dish and leave to soak in the mixture for a few seconds, then turn it over and soak until moist.

**3** Put the soaked bread in the pan, repeat with another slice of bread and fry for 2–3 minutes on each side until lightly browned. Transfer to a plate and keep warm in the oven while you make the rest of the French toast. Serve warm.

# cornbread pudding

My grandmother created this delicious breakfast 'pudding'. It's so moreish that it's hard to stop eating once you start, especially warm from the oven.

**SERVES:**
2 adults and
2 children

**PREPARATION TIME:**
20 minutes

**COOKING TIME:**
45 minutes

**STORAGE:**
Refrigerate for
up to 3 days.

55g/2oz butter, cubed,
   plus extra for greasing
150g/5½oz/1 cup polenta
115g/4oz/½ cup sugar
375ml/13fl oz/1½ cups
   rice milk
2 eggs, beaten
1 tsp gluten-free baking
   powder
¼ tsp salt

**1** Preheat the oven to 180°C/350°F/Gas 4 and grease a 20 x 20cm/ 8 x 8in baking dish with butter. Put the polenta in a large mixing bowl and whisk in 455ml/16fl oz/scant 2 cups boiling water, using a wire whisk.

**2** Add the butter and sugar and mix with a spoon or rubber spatula until smooth and there are no lumps. Add the rice milk, eggs, baking powder and salt and mix well. Pour into the baking dish.

**3** Bake for 45 minutes until golden brown and firm at the edges. It will be wobbly in the middle. Remove from the oven and leave to cool for 10 minutes, then slice and serve hot, warm or cold.

*rice milk*
is an excellent
substitute for cow's
milk in baking.
Made from brown rice,
it has a lovely
natural sweetness.

# ▲ squash & potato soup

This is a quick and easy soup that's perfect on a crisp autumn day. Children love the velvety texture, bright colour and gentle sweetness.

**SERVES:**
2 adults and
2 children

**PREPARATION
TIME:**
15 minutes

**COOKING TIME:**
30 minutes

**STORAGE:**
Refrigerate for
up to 3 days or
freeze for up to
3 months.

1 small butternut squash,
   peeled, deseeded and
   cubed
2 potatoes, unpeeled
   and cubed
2 onions, chopped
2 garlic cloves, roughly
   chopped
⅛ tsp cayenne pepper
455ml/16fl oz/scant
   2 cups vegetable stock
80ml/2½fl oz/¼ cup olive
   oil

1 Put the squash, potatoes, onions, garlic, cayenne pepper and vegetable stock in a large saucepan and bring to the boil over a medium-high heat. Reduce the heat to medium-low and simmer, covered, for 30 minutes until the squash and potatoes are soft.

2 Using an immersion blender, purée the mixture for 1–2 minutes until creamy but still chunky. Add the olive oil and serve hot.

*cayenne
pepper*
stimulates digestive
juices and is healing to
stomach tissues and other
digestive organs, making
it much gentler on the
body than black
pepper.

# tomato soup with rice

There's nothing like homemade tomato soup and, served over rice, it makes a filling meal. Roasting the tomatoes creates a deep, rich flavour.

**MAKES:**
4 servings

**PREPARATION TIME:**
20 minutes, plus at least 7 hours soaking

**COOKING TIME:**
1 hour 30 minutes

**STORAGE:**
Refrigerate the soup for up to 3 days or freeze for up to 3 months. Refrigerate the rice for up to 1 day. Reheat until hot.

175g/6oz/1 cup brown basmati rice
1 tbsp kefir or natural yogurt
12 tomatoes, about 1.5kg/3lb 5oz, halved
6 garlic cloves, quartered lengthways
1 large onion, chopped
4 tbsp olive oil
vegetable bouillon powder for 500ml/17fl oz/2 cups water, according to packet instructions
455ml/16fl oz/scant 2 cups vegetable stock

**1** Put the rice, kefir and 500ml/17fl oz/2 cups warm water in a medium saucepan and leave to soak, covered, for 7 hours or overnight.

**2** Preheat the oven to 200°C/400°F/Gas 6. Make a small triangular cut in the stem-end of each tomato half to remove the hard part. Put the tomatoes, cut-side up, in a large baking tray and top each one with 1 slice of garlic. Sprinkle the onion and oil over the tomatoes and bake for 1 hour until they start to brown.

**3** While the tomatoes are baking, bring the rice to the boil over a high heat. Stir in enough the vegetable bouillon powder, then reduce the heat to low and cook, covered, for 30 minutes until the rice is just tender.

**4** Remove the tomatoes from the oven and transfer them to a large saucepan. Add the vegetable stock and bring to a simmer over a medium-high heat, then reduce the heat to low and simmer for 30 minutes, stirring occasionally, until the tomatoes are soft. Blend the mixture with an immersion blender for 2–3 minutes until completely smooth.

**5** Divide the rice into four bowls and pour the soup over. Serve hot.

*tomato skins* are an excellent source not only of fibre but also of flavanoids, a powerful antioxidant, so I never remove them. They purée when you blend the soup, and they help to deepen the flavour of the dish.

# creamy rustic soup

This is a great soup for kids because it's substantial enough to be a meal. It's especially good in the autumn or winter.

SERVES:
2 adults and
2 children

PREPARATION
TIME:
25 minutes,
plus overnight
soaking

COOKING TIME:
1 hour 45 minutes

STORAGE:
Refrigerate for
up to 3 days or
freeze for up to
3 months.

100g/3½oz/½ cup pearl
  barley
55g/2oz/⅓ cup spelt
70g/2½oz/⅓ cup split
  red lentils
70g/2½oz/⅓ cup mung
  beans
1 strip of kombu, about
  15 x 5cm/6 x 2in, cut
  into little pieces
5 tbsp olive oil
2 onions, chopped
6 garlic cloves, quartered
2 carrots, quartered
  lengthways, then cut
  into 5mm/¼in-thick
  pieces
2 large tomatoes,
  chopped
3 tbsp vegetable bouillon
  powder
Tabasco sauce, to serve
  (optional)

1 Put the barley, spelt, red lentils and mung beans in a large bowl, cover with warm water and leave to soak, covered, overnight.

2 Drain the soaked grain and bean mixture in a sieve and rinse well under cold running water, then transfer to a large saucepan. Add 1.5l/52fl oz/6 cups water and bring to the boil over a high heat. Boil for 10 minutes, skimming any scum that rises to the surface, then add the kombu. Reduce the heat to medium-low and simmer, covered, for 45 minutes until the grains and beans are soft, then discard the kombu.

3 Meanwhile, heat a small saucepan over a medium heat. Add 1 tablespoon of the olive oil and when it is hot, add the onions and garlic. Cook for 10 minutes, stirring frequently, until brown, then set aside.

4 When the grain and bean mixture is cooked, add the onions and garlic along with the carrots, tomatoes and vegetable bouillon. Simmer, covered, over a low heat for a further 1 hour, stirring occasionally, until the vegetables are very tender.

5 Divide the soup into four bowls and drizzle each portion with 1 tablespoon of the remaining olive oil. Season the adult portions with the Tabasco sauce, if using. Serve hot.

*barley*
adds a richness of
flavour plus a good dose
of nutrients and fibre to
a warming wintry stew. It
also provides fuel for the
liver and muscles, and
helps to keep your
baby regular.

# baked beans with jacket potatoes

**SERVES:**
2 adults and
2 children

**PREPARATION TIME:**
35 minutes, plus overnight soaking

**COOKING TIME:**
3 hours

**STORAGE:**
Refrigerate the beans for up to 3 days or freeze for up to 3 months.

Nicholas and Cassie love the slightly sweet, piquant flavour of these baked beans. You'll be surprised how amazing and delicious they are—and how completely different from processed versions. This recipe makes twice as many beans as you need, but serve them over the next few days with eggs or on toast and they'll quickly disappear.

450g/1lb/2 cups dried haricot beans
2 tsp lemon juice
2 strips of kombu, each about 15 x 5cm/6 x 2in, cut into tiny pieces
2 onions, chopped
4 garlic cloves, crushed in a garlic press
3 tbsp olive oil
2 tbsp molasses
2 tsp non-hot mustard
3 tbsp tomato purée
4 baking potatoes, pierced with a fork
2 tsp salt

**1** Put the beans and lemon juice in a large saucepan, cover with warm water and leave to soak, covered, overnight.

**2** Drain and rinse the beans. Return them to the pan and add 1.25l/44fl oz/5 cups water. Bring to the boil over a high heat and boil for 10 minutes, skimming any scum that rises to the surface. Reduce the heat to low, add the kombu and simmer, covered, for 1 hour until the beans are soft, then discard the kombu.

**3** Preheat the oven to 150°C/300°F/Gas 2. Transfer the beans and cooking liquid to a deep, covered casserole dish. Add the onions, garlic, olive oil, molasses, mustard and tomato purée and mix well. There should be enough liquid to just cover the beans; if not, add a little extra water. If the beans are cold by the time you are ready to put them in the oven, bring the mixture to a simmer in the casserole over a medium-high heat on the hob.

**4** Put the beans and the potatoes in the oven and bake, covered, for 2 hours, then remove them from the oven. Stir the salt into the beans.

**5** Cut open the potatoes, top each one with a few tablespoons of the beans and serve.

*potatoes*
have just about every nutrient, except for vitamin A. For optimum nutrition, eat them with their skins on. Cut away and discard any green parts; these form when potatoes are exposed to light, increasing the levels of solanine, a toxin.

# grilled cherry tomato spaghetti ▶

Grilling makes cherry tomatoes even more delicious – and soft and sloppy to mix with pasta. Children and adults will love this quick meal, which is perfect for when there's a lot of hunger, but not a lot of time.

**SERVES:**
2 adults and
2 children

**PREPARATION TIME:**
5 minutes

**COOKING TIME:**
15 minutes

**STORAGE:**
Not suitable
for storage.

salt
300g/10½oz dried
    wholemeal spelt
    spaghetti
250g/9oz cherry tomatoes
olive oil, to serve

**1** Preheat the grill to medium. Bring a large pan of salted water to the boil and cook the spaghetti according to the packet instructions.

**2** While the spaghetti is cooking, put the tomatoes in a baking dish and grill for 5 minutes until lightly browned and beginning to pop. Remove from under the grill.

**3** Drain the spaghetti and divide it into four bowls. Spoon the tomatoes over the top and drizzle with a generous amount of olive oil. Season with salt and serve immediately.

# mashed potato craters

A gorgeous way to eat potatoes, this dish is also fun for kids. For variation, you can substitute the olive oil with butter or gravy. A hearty mixed salad is a great accompaniment.

**SERVES:**
2 adults and
2 children

**PREPARATION TIME:**
15 minutes

**COOKING TIME:**
20 minutes

**STORAGE:**
Not suitable
for storage.

1kg/2lb 4oz potatoes, cut
    into 2cm/¾in cubes
2 carrots, cut into
    1cm/½in cubes
3 garlic cloves
½ tsp salt
4 tbsp olive oil

**1** Put the potatoes, carrots and garlic in a steamer and steam, covered, over boiling water for 20 minutes until the potatoes and carrots are soft. Remove from the heat and transfer to a medium bowl, reserving the steam water.

**2** Add the salt and a little of the steam water and blend, using an immersion blender, for 1–2 minutes until smooth and creamy. Add additional steam water if needed.

**3** Using a tablespoon, divide the mixture onto four plates, mounding each portion up into a mountain. The two adult portions should be twice as big as the two child portions. Using a teaspoon, hollow a crater into the top of each mountain. Pour 4 teaspoons of the olive oil into the adult portions and 2 teaspoons into the child portions. Serve immediately.

# wholegrain risotto with asparagus

This nutty, brown-rice risotto has added appeal because of the fresh, lightly steamed asparagus. My kids love the creaminess of this dish and the little bite-sized asparagus logs.

**SERVES:**
2 adults and 2 children

**PREPARATION TIME:**
15 minutes, plus at least 7 hours soaking

**COOKING TIME:**
1 hour 10 minutes

**STORAGE:**
Not suitable for storage.

**200g/7oz/1 cup brown Arborio rice**
**1 tsp kefir or natural yogurt**
**200g/7oz asparagus, cut into 2cm/¾in pieces**
**500ml/17fl oz/2 cups vegetable stock**
**30g/1oz butter**
**3 tbsp olive oil**
**1 onion, finely chopped**

**1** Put the rice, kefir and enough warm water to cover in a medium saucepan and soak, covered, for 7 hours or overnight, then drain.

**2** Put the asparagus in a steamer and steam, covered, over boiling water for 3–5 minutes until just tender, then remove from the heat and set aside. Meanwhile, put the vegetable stock in a medium saucepan. Add 500ml/17fl oz/2 cups water and bring to a simmer over a medium heat.

**3** Heat a large frying pan over a medium-low heat and add the rice. Heat for 10 minutes, stirring frequently, until the rice has dried, then transfer it to a dry bowl. Put the butter and oil in the frying pan and increase the heat to medium. When the butter has melted, add the onion and cook for 10 minutes, stirring occasionally with a wooden spoon, until translucent. Add the rice and stir for 3 minutes until the grains are coated and glossy.

**4** Reduce the heat to medium-low. Add 1 ladleful of the stock to the rice and cook for 3–4 minutes, stirring continuously, until the stock has been absorbed. Then add another ladleful of the stock, repeating this process until all of the stock has been added. This will take 35–40 minutes. Make sure to keep the risotto at a very gentle simmer, reducing the heat to low if necessary. When all of the liquid has been absorbed, the rice will be creamy and slightly chewy.

**5** Stir in the asparagus and cook for another 3 minutes to warm it through. Serve immediately.

*asparagus*
is a natural diuretic that contributes to healthy gut flora. It's also good for the heart. Besides that, asparagus is simply delicious. Your baby will love it paired with other foods or lightly steamed on its own.

# chicken & mushroom pasta

Adding raw, grated vegetables to a dish is a great way to increase your child's intake of vitamins and minerals. They also add freshness and flavour.

SERVES:
2 adults and
2 children

PREPARATION TIME:
15 minutes

COOKING TIME:
25 minutes

STORAGE:
Refrigerate for up to 2 days.

55g/2oz butter
400g/14oz boneless, skinless chicken breast
225g/8oz/3 cups dried wholemeal spelt pasta shells
100g/3½oz button mushrooms, chopped
1 small carrot, grated
2 tbsp olive oil
salt

**1** Melt half of the butter in a small frying pan over a medium-high heat. Season both sides of the chicken with salt and add it to the pan. Cook, covered, for 5 minutes on each side until cooked through. Transfer the chicken to a plate and leave to cool, then cut it into bite-sized pieces.

**2** Bring a large saucepan of salted water to the boil and cook the pasta according to the packet instructions, then drain and transfer to a medium-sized serving bowl.

**3** Meanwhile, melt the remaining butter in the same frying pan over a medium-low heat. Add the mushrooms and fry for 10 minutes, stirring occasionally, until lightly browned.

**4** Add the chicken, mushrooms, carrot and olive oil to the pasta and toss well. Serve warm.

# best beef burgers ▶

My dad loved beef burgers when I was growing up – thrown on the barbecue from spring to autumn and cooked inside in the winter. The chopped onion transforms ordinary burgers into a wonderful treat.

SERVES:
2 adults and
2 children

PREPARATION TIME:
10 minutes

COOKING TIME:
10 minutes

STORAGE:
Refrigerate uncooked burgers for up to 2 days or freeze for up to 1 month.

450g/1lb/2½ cups beef mince
1 small onion, finely chopped
1 tbsp olive oil
salt and freshly ground black pepper

To serve (optional):
3 wholemeal spelt hamburger buns
lettuce
sliced tomato
sliced gherkins

**1** Put the mince and onion in a medium bowl and mix well. Shape some of the mixture into 4 small patties, about 5cm/2in wide and 2cm/¾in high, for child portions. Shape the remaining mixture into 2 patties, about 9cm/3½in wide and 2cm/¾in high, for adult portions. Season with salt and pepper and put the patties on a plate.

**2** Heat a large frying pan over a medium-high heat. Add the oil and when it is hot, put the burgers in the pan. Fry, partially covered, for 4–5 minutes on each side until the burgers are crispy and brown. Serve hot. Adults may enjoy this on a wholemeal bun with lettuce, tomato and gherkin, while little mouths will need theirs served with one-quarter or one-half of a bun and the vegetables, if desired.

# 15 to 24 months

This is the moment the whole family has been waiting for. Once your baby is eating the foods introduced in the chart on page 91, he can eat all family meals. This will really simplify your cooking routine, but you might find yourself shrinking your repertoire of foods back down now that he's eating with you. If you haven't already, make an extra effort to turn the kind of cooking you have been doing for him into a habit, and everyone will be eating well. The recipes in this chapter will help you do this. It features delicious dishes that will appeal to older children and adults as much as they appeal to your toddler. There's a great mix of options here, using all sorts of ingredients, most of which you're very familiar with by now. Keep trying new things, though, to ensure a good mix of flavours and nutrients in your diet – and you'll find new foods that you and your child will love. Remember to continue using salt very sparingly in your cooking, and avoid sugar as much as possible.

**CHEESE:** You can introduce cheese now, but it's good to offer a variety – not only cow's milk cheeses. Sheep's and goat's milk cheeses are best and, of course, organic is heaps better than conventional because there are no antibiotic or pesticide residues to worry about and no growth hormones that could interfere with your child's normal development. Definitely avoid processed cheeses. If you look at the labels on these 'cheese products', you'll see that they include all sorts of additives. Don't waste any of your child's – or your own – calories on them.

**WHEAT:** At this age, you can introduce wheat, but be careful not to rely on it too much. Spelt and Kamut are much better options, and rotating different grains other than those in the wheat family, such as quinoa and millet, is much healthier for all of you. When you buy pasta, don't habitually reach for the wheat versions. The pastas introduced in the first half of this chapter did not include wheat, and there are so many other kinds available. Opt for rice, corn, buckwheat, spelt and Kamut pastas, and try the different varieties of Japanese noodles available as well. Adding wheat to your child's diet makes it much easier to eat out in restaurants. Most menus feature a pasta dish, which can be great for kids. Restaurants don't usually offer wholemeal pasta, but eating white flour occasionally is fine, so don't worry about allowing your child to eat white pasta when you're out. Just make sure you continue to make whole grains a big part of his diet when you're cooking for him at home.

**BREADS:** Another great thing about introducing wheat is that you can get more creative with the breads you offer. Give him a variety of different flavours and textures.

Try sourdough rye, Irish soda bread, sprouted breads and spelt bread (there are two great spelt bread recipes in this book, see pages 142 and 153). All of these breads taste different and provide your growing toddler with a range of different nutrients.

VEGETABLES: When cooking vegetables now, you can do them *al dente* so that they are still firm. This keeps more of the nutrition intact. And remember not to peel vegetables so that your child gets all of the fibre and the full range of nutrients. It's good to offer at least two types of vegetables at each meal. I like to serve different colours, with one cooked and one raw. I'm not really into making shapes with food because children naturally like food if it is fresh and well cooked. It can be fun, however, to take a few moments and arrange vegetables into pretty patterns or pictures on the plate.

DRINKS: As mentioned in chapter 3, avoid offering lots of fruit juices. Fruits start to lose nutritional value after juicing, so unless you're juicing at home, most juices don't have much nutrition. It's better to not let children get used to having sweet drinks, anyway. Instead, keep giving your child water to drink. It's a great habit to get into. If he does want a fruity drink, make a smoothie for an afternoon snack. Just throw some chopped fruit

## NEW FOODS TO INTRODUCE AT 15–24 MONTHS
*Your child is now ready for the foods listed in the chart below. Combine them with the foods listed in the previous charts to give him the best variety you can.*

| FRUITS | VEGETABLES | GRAINS | NUTS & SEEDS | DAIRY & EGGS |
|---|---|---|---|---|
| • grapefruit<br>• orange | • Brussels sprout<br>• samphire<br>• seaweed (all types, including arame, hijiki, kombu and nori) | • wheat | • nuts:<br>almond<br>Brazil nut<br>chestnut<br>hazelnut<br>macadamia nut<br>pecan<br>pine nut<br>pistachio nut<br>walnut | • cheese, especially organic goat's and sheep's milk |

into your blender along with yogurt, rice milk or oat milk, blend until smooth and serve. Smoothies are naturally sweet, so you never need to add sugar. Or offer a piece of fruit. He'll get better nutrition from eating an apple than from drinking apple juice.

**NUTS & SEEDS:** Now that your baby is chewing well, he can start to eat seeds, not just seed oil. He can also have nuts, which are loaded with healthy fats. Chop them up or grind them in a spice mill first, then mix them in with his breakfast cereal or with raisins for a snack. Nut and seed butters are great, too. You can sandwich them between rice cakes or cripsbreads for a convenient snack when you're on the go. Don't rely too heavily on peanut butter, though, and if you are using it, make sure to buy organic. Non-organic peanuts are one of the most pesticide-laden crops, so you don't want your child exposed to all that chemical residue. Peanuts are also often contaminated with moulds that produce aflatoxins, which may be carcinogenic. If there is any family history of nut allergies, wait until age five to introduce them.

**ESSENTIAL FATTY-ACID (EFA) SEED MIX:** Make a seed mix to have to hand. Put one measure each of sesame seeds and your choice of either sunflower or pumpkin seeds in a jar. Add two measures of flax seeds, seal tightly and keep in the fridge away from light, heat and air. Grind two tablespoons of the mixture in a spice mill at mealtime and mix it into your baby's food. Alternate this with the oils for a nice change and more texture.

**CITRUS FRUIT:** Oranges and grapefruit are the last fruits I introduce because they are very common allergenic foods. At this age, your child should be able to handle them. Include these fruits in your child's diet occasionally, but make sure to keep giving him lots of other kinds, too. As with other fruit juices, don't let him consume orange juice regularly because he'll want that sweet flavour all the time. It's always better to fill up on food rather than liquids anyway. Once your child is eating these fruits, he can now eat any fruit.

**EATING ENOUGH:** Again, don't worry if you think he's not eating enough. If he's already feeding himself but you really want to get him to eat more, wait until he's finished, then put some toys on the table. While he's distracted by the toys, you can carry on feeding him some more until he is really full. However, one solid meal a day is usually enough between fifteen months and two years. If he's hungry and wants more food, he'll make sure you know it.

Your little one will still need you to cut up most of the dishes that follow. If he isn't chewing enough yet, just wait a little longer and make these recipes when he's older. Also, in the following pages there are recipes for things like hummus, tomato sauce and black bean soup. These delicious recipes are great to make when you have some extra time – they're always good to have around for snacks and quick meals when you don't have that much time to cook.

# MEAL PLANNER FOR TODDLERS AT 15–24 MONTHS

*Follow this meal planner as closely as you can without stressing out. For variation, you can alternate seed oils with 2 teaspoons of ground EFA Seed Mix (see page 92).*

| DAY | BREAKFAST | MID-MORNING | LUNCH | MID-AFTERNOON | TEA |
|---|---|---|---|---|---|
| 1 | toasted wholemeal pitta with tahini | fruit (fresh or dried) | Cheese & Onion Rye Toasts (see page 97)<br>raw carrot<br>steamed broccoli with 2 tsp seed oil | corn cakes | Roasted Veggies with Feta (see page 95)<br>grilled chicken |
| 2 | porridge with raisins and yogurt | fruit (fresh or dried) | Lemon Mackerel Mayo & Cucumber Sandwiches (see page 104)<br>sweetcorn | oatcakes | No-Meat Meatballs (see page 100) with spaghetti and tomato sauce<br>sprouts and lettuce with 2 tsp seed oil |
| 3 | wholemeal rye toast with almond butter | fruit (fresh or dried) | Hummus, Sprouts & Avocado (see page 97)<br>cottage cheese | wholemeal rye crackers/crispbreads | Baked Frittata (see page 99)<br>steamed cauliflower with 2 tsp seed oil |
| 4 | Mustard Scrambled Eggs (see page 78)<br>spelt toast | fruit (fresh or dried) | Arame Rice with Toasted Seeds (see page 105)<br>steamed artichoke hearts with 2 tsp seed oil | low-salt popcorn | Tuna Pie (see page 107)<br>raw fennel |
| 5 | muesli soaked overnight with rice milk | fruit (fresh or dried) | Polenta with Shiitake Mushrooms (see page 98) | Japanese brown rice crackers | Quesadillas (see page 101)<br>Butternut Squash Purée (see page 30) with 2 tsp EFA Seed Mix (see page 92) |
| 6 | puffed rice (no added sugar) with yogurt | fruit (fresh or dried) | Sweetcorn & Pea Pancakes (see page 100)<br>sardines | wholemeal grissini or pretzels | Spinach Bake (see page 103)<br>Cucumber & Tomato Salad (see page 151) with 2 tsp EFA Seed Mix (see page 92) |
| 7 | rye toast with mayonnaise and smoked salmon | fruit (fresh or dried) | Kamut Pasta with Veggies & Walnuts (see page 104)<br>Rocket & Lemon Salad (see page 150) | low-salt, baked tortillas | Black Bean Soup with Rice (see page 94)<br>beetroot with 2 tsp seed oil |

# black bean soup with rice

An old family recipe from my mom, this soup has a simplicity that belies its flavour. Kids like it so much that, if you have a large freezer, it's worth making batches of the soup and then freezing it.

**SERVES:**
4 adults and
4 children

**PREPARATION TIME:**
20 minutes,
plus overnight
soaking

**COOKING TIME:**
2 hours 10 minutes

**STORAGE:**
Refrigerate the
soup for up to
3 days or freeze for
up to 3 months.
Refrigerate the rice
for up to 1 day.
Reheat until hot.

*slow cooking*
fresh, wholesome
ingredients at a low
temperature for a long time
creates a delicious, nutritious
meal with meltingly tender
components – and as with this
soup, the goodness from the
vegetables and pulses
stays in the pot.

500g/1lb 2oz/2½ cups dried black turtle beans
2 tsp lemon juice
175g/6oz/2 cups brown basmati rice
1 tbsp kefir or natural yogurt
1 strip of kombu, about 15 x 5cm/6 x 2in, cut into little pieces
1 large onion, finely chopped
170ml/5½fl oz/⅔ cup olive oil
70ml/2¼fl oz/scant ⅓ cup white wine vinegar
5 garlic cloves, crushed
1 yellow pepper, deseeded and chopped
½ tsp dried oregano
1 tbsp ground cumin
4 tsp salt
Tabasco sauce, to serve (optional)

1 Put the beans and lemon juice in a large saucepan, cover with warm water and leave to soak, covered, overnight.

2 Put the rice, kefir and 1l/35fl oz/4 cups warm water in a medium saucepan and leave to soak, covered, for 7 hours or overnight.

3 Drain and rinse the beans. Return them to the pan and add 2l/70fl oz/8 cups water. Bring to the boil over a high heat and boil for 10 minutes, skimming any scum that rises to the surface. Reduce the heat to low, add the kombu and simmer, covered, for 1 hour until the beans are soft.

4 When the beans have cooked halfway, bring the rice to the boil over a high heat, then reduce the heat to low and cook, covered, for 30 minutes until just tender. As soon as the rice has finished cooking, remove it from the heat and stir in half of the onion, 3 tablespoons of the olive oil and 2 teaspoons of the vinegar. Set aside and leave to marinate for 1 hour or until the soup is ready.

5 Add the garlic, yellow pepper, oregano, cumin and the remaining onion to the beans. Stir in the remaining 4 tablespoons vinegar and continue cooking, covered, for a further 1 hour, stirring occasionally, until the beans are very soft. Stir in the salt and the remaining 125ml/4fl oz/½ cup of the olive oil.

6 Put some of the rice in four bowls and top with 1 ladleful of the soup. Season the adult portions with the Tabasco sauce, if using. Serve hot.

# ▼ roasted veggies with feta

The roasted garlic combined with rosemary and browned feta cheese in this dish makes a fabulous mix. Children love the different-coloured vegetables, which are sweet and delicious when roasted.

SERVES:
2 adults and
2 children

PREPARATION
TIME:
20 minutes

COOKING TIME:
25 minutes

STORAGE:
Refrigerate for
up to 3 days.

4 tbsp olive oil
375g/13oz potatoes, cut into small cubes
1 carrot, quartered lengthways and sliced into rounds
10 garlic cloves
½ tsp dried rosemary
100g/3½oz broccoli, cut into bite-sized florets
1 small red pepper, deseeded and cut into small pieces
175g/6oz feta cheese, cut into small cubes

1 Preheat the oven to 250°C/500°F/Gas 9 and grease a medium baking dish with 1 tablespoon of the olive oil. Put the potatoes, carrot, garlic, rosemary and 2 tablespoons of the remaining olive oil in a large bowl and mix well, then pour them into the baking dish. Bake for 15 minutes until the vegetables are beginning to soften.

2 Meanwhile, put the broccoli, red pepper, feta cheese and remaining 1 tablespoon of olive oil in another bowl and mix well.

3 Remove the vegetables from the oven and stir in the broccoli mixture. Bake for a further 10 minutes until the vegetables and feta are beginning to brown. Serve hot.

# ◄ hummus, sprouts & avocado

This is a delicious reminder of why hummus is great to have in the fridge – and when you make your own, you control how much salt goes into it.

**SERVES:**
2 adults and 2 children

**PREPARATION TIME:**
20 minutes, plus overnight soaking

**COOKING TIME:**
2 hours 10 minutes

**STORAGE:**
Refrigerate the hummus for up to 3 days.

100g/3½oz/½ cup dried chickpeas
3 tbsp plus 2 tsp lemon juice
1 strip of kombu, about 8 x 5cm/3¼ x 2in
2 garlic cloves, crushed
1 tbsp tahini
4 tbsp olive oil
¼ tsp salt
6 slices of wholemeal spelt bread
2 avocados, halved, pitted and peeled, then sliced
55g/2oz alfalfa sprouts
½ lemon, cut into 4 wedges

**1** Put the chickpeas and 2 teaspoons of the lemon juice in a medium saucepan, cover with warm water and leave to soak, covered, overnight.

**2** Drain and rinse the chickpeas and return them to the pan. Add 670ml/23fl oz/2⅔ cups water and bring to the boil over a high heat. Boil for 10 minutes, skimming any scum that rises to the surface, then reduce the heat to low, add the kombu and cook, covered, for 2 hours until soft. Remove from the heat and leave the chickpeas to cool completely in the cooking water.

**3** Drain and rinse well, then put the chickpeas and kombu in a blender. Add the garlic, tahini, olive oil, salt, remaining lemon juice and 4 tablespoons water. Blend for 1–2 minutes until smooth.

**4** Toast the bread and then spread 1 tablespoon of the hummus on each slice and top with a few slices of the avocado. Divide the sprouts over the avocado, then squeeze the lemon wedges over. Cut into strips and serve immediately.

# cheese & onion rye toasts

This is a cross between an American grilled cheese sandwich and English cheese on toast. The red onion softens while the cheese melts underneath, creating a flavour and texture that your little ones will find delightful.

**SERVES:**
2 adults and 2 children

**PREPARATION TIME:**
10 minutes

**COOKING TIME:**
4 minutes

**STORAGE:**
Not suitable for storage.

6 slices of wholemeal rye bread
non-hot mustard, to taste, for spreading
175g/6oz mature Cheddar cheese, cut into 5mm/¼in-thick slices
1 red onion, sliced into rings and quartered

**1** Preheat the grill to medium. Meanwhile, toast the bread in a toaster, then spread a little mustard on one side of each slice and put them on a large baking sheet. Divide the cheese over the toasts, covering well, then evenly arrange the onion over the cheese.

**2** Grill for 4 minutes until the onion has softened and the cheese is beginning to melt. Serve hot.

# polenta with shiitake mushrooms

SERVES:
2 adults and
2 children

PREPARATION TIME:
15 minutes

COOKING TIME:
45 minutes

STORAGE:
Refrigerate the polenta and mushrooms separately for up to 3 days.

Polenta is wonderfully versatile, and children love its subtle, sweet flavour. When you feel like experimenting, try mixing in extra ingredients, such as six whole garlic cloves, a chopped onion, and/or grated cheese, in step 1.

**30g/1oz butter, plus extra for greasing**
**175g/6oz/1 cup polenta**
**1 tsp salt**
**1 onion, finely chopped**
**1 garlic clove, finely chopped**
**1 tsp dried thyme**
**450g/1lb shiitake mushrooms, brushed clean, stems discarded and caps sliced**
**185ml/6fl oz/¾ cup Greek yogurt**

**1** Grease a 30cm/12in round baking dish with butter and set aside. Put 875ml/30fl oz/3½ cups water in a heavy-based saucepan and bring to the boil over a high heat. Reduce the heat to medium and pour in the polenta, whisking continuously with a metal whisk until smooth. Stir in the salt and then reduce the heat to low. Cook for 15 minutes, stirring continuously with a wooden spoon until the polenta is thick and rubbery, then pour it into the baking dish and smooth the top using a rubber spatula. Leave to cool and set.

**2** While the polenta is cooling, make the mushroom mixture. Melt the butter in a large frying pan over a medium-high heat. Add the onion and cook for 5 minutes, stirring, until lightly browned. Add the garlic and thyme and continue cooking for a further 3 minutes, stirring occasionally.

**3** Increase the heat to high and add the mushrooms. Cook for 10 minutes, stirring continuously, until the mushrooms are golden brown. Remove from the heat and stir in the yogurt, then set aside.

**4** Preheat the grill to medium. Cut the polenta into 8 wedges and grill in the baking dish for 5 minutes until warm and crisp.

**5** Divide the grilled polenta onto plates and spoon 2 tablespoons of the mushroom mixture over the tops. Serve immediately.

*shiitake mushrooms*
have a potent flavour and have been used medicinally by the Chinese for more than 6,000 years. They contain an active compound called lentinan, which strengthens the immune system so it can fight infection and disease.

# ▾ baked frittata

A frittata is a type of Italian omelette that often includes meats, cheeses and vegetables. It is usually cooked on the hob and finished under the grill.

**SERVES:**
2 adults and
2 children

**PREPARATION TIME:**
15 minutes

**COOKING TIME:**
55 minutes

**STORAGE:**
Refrigerate for
up to 3 days.

butter, for greasing
350g/12oz red potatoes,
   unpeeled, chopped into
   1.5cm/⅝in cubes
2 tsp olive oil
1 onion, chopped
5 eggs, beaten
120g/4¼oz frozen
   spinach, chopped
175g/6oz feta cheese,
   cut into 1cm/½in cubes
55g/2oz/½ cup pitted
   Kalamata olives, cut
   into rings
Tabasco sauce (optional),
   to serve

**1** Preheat the oven to 200°C/400°F/Gas 6 and generously grease a large pie plate or round baking dish with butter. Bring a large saucepan of water to the boil and cook the potatoes for 10 minutes or until soft. Remove from the heat, drain and leave to cool.

**2** Heat the oil in a medium frying pan over a medium heat. When the oil is hot, add the onion and cook for 10 minutes, stirring occasionally, until brown. Stir in the potatoes, eggs, spinach, feta and olives and mix well, then pour the mixture into the baking dish. Bake for 25–30 minutes until the egg is just cooked.

**3** Meanwhile, preheat the grill to medium. Transfer the baking dish to the top shelf under the grill and grill for 3 minutes until the cheese is lightly browned. Serve hot with the Tabasco sauce, if using.

# no-meat meatballs

These succulent tofu balls are a delicious alternative to meatballs.

**SERVES:**
2 adults and 2 children

**PREPARATION TIME:**
30 minutes, plus making the tomato sauce

**COOKING TIME:**
35 minutes

**STORAGE:**
Refrigerate for up to 2 days.

2 tsp olive oil, plus extra for greasing
1 small onion, chopped
2 slices of wholemeal wheat or spelt bread, lightly toasted
400g/14oz firm tofu, drained
3 eggs, beaten
40g/1½oz Cheddar cheese, grated
¼ tsp salt, plus extra for cooking the pasta
1 tsp dried oregano
300g/10½oz dried spelt pasta
½ recipe quantity Tomato Sauce (see page 117)

**1** Preheat the oven to 180°C/350°F/Gas 4 and grease a large baking dish with olive oil. Heat the olive oil in a small frying pan over a medium-high heat, add the onion and cook for 5 minutes, stirring occasionally, until beginning to soften. Meanwhile, lightly toast the bread, then put it in a blender and blend for 1 minute until breadcrumbs form.

**2** Crumble the tofu into a large bowl. Add the breadcrumbs, onion, eggs, Cheddar, salt and oregano and mix well with a fork.

**3** Shape the mixture into 20 balls of equal size and put them in the baking dish. Bake for 30 minutes. Meanwhile, bring a large pan of salted water to the boil and cook the pasta according to the packet instructions, then drain and transfer to a serving bowl. Heat the tomato sauce and serve hot with the pasta and no-meat meatballs.

# sweetcorn & pea pancakes

These simple, savoury pancakes are a great way to get your child to eat his peas. They're good on their own, but for variation try them served with yogurt on the side or with grated cheese sprinkled on top.

**SERVES:**
2 adults and 2 children

**PREPARATION TIME:**
10 minutes

**COOKING TIME:**
20 minutes

**STORAGE:**
Refrigerate the cooked pancakes for up to 3 days.

125g/4½oz/1 cup wholemeal spelt flour
1 tsp baking powder
2 eggs, beaten
150ml/5fl oz/scant ⅔ cup milk
85g/3oz/¾ cup peas
85g/3oz/¾ cup sweetcorn
½ tsp salt
1 tsp olive oil

**1** Preheat the oven to 70°C/150°F/Gas ¼. Put the flour and baking powder in a medium bowl and mix well. Whisk in the eggs and milk until smooth and then stir in the peas, sweetcorn and salt.

**2** Heat the olive oil in a large frying pan over a medium-low heat until hot. Pour tablespoonfuls of the batter into the pan, spacing well apart, and cook for 2–3 minutes on each side until lightly browned. Alternatively, cook the pancakes on a griddle over a medium-low heat for 2–3 minutes on each side until lightly browned. Transfer to a plate and keep warm in the oven while you make the remaining pancakes. Serve hot.

# quesadillas

Quesadillas are so quick to make – and I haven't yet met a child who doesn't like them. You can lift the flavour by sprinkling some sliced spring onions over the cheese.

**SERVES:**
2 adults and
2 children

**PREPARATION TIME:**
10 minutes, plus overnight soaking

**COOKING TIME:**
1 hour 40 minutes

**STORAGE:**
Refrigerate the beans for up to 3 days.

100g/3½oz/½ cup dried adzuki beans
2 tsp lemon juice
1 strip of kombu, about 8 x 5cm/3¼ x 2in, cut into little pieces
½ tsp salt
175g/6oz Cheddar cheese, grated
12 flour tortillas

**1** Put the beans and lemon juice in a medium saucepan, cover with warm water and leave to soak, covered, overnight.

**2** Drain and rinse the beans. Return them to the pan and add 750ml/26fl oz/3 cups water. Bring to the boil over a high heat and boil for 10 minutes, skimming any scum that rises to the surface. Reduce the heat to low, add the kombu and cook, covered, for 1 hour until the beans are soft. Check occasionally to ensure that the beans remain covered with water and add extra boiling water if necessary. Drain well, then return to the pan and stir in the salt.

**3** Preheat the oven to 70°C/150°F/Gas ¼. Heat a large frying pan over a medium heat until hot. Put 1 tortilla in the pan, sprinkle with 15g/½oz of the Cheddar followed by a few tablespoons of the beans and then another 15g/½oz of the Cheddar. Cover with a second tortilla and cook for 3–4 minutes until the underside of the bottom tortilla is lightly browned and the cheese has melted.

**4** Slide a spatula under the tortilla and put your fingertips on top of the top tortilla, then flip it over and cook the other side for 3 minutes until lightly browned. Slide the quesadilla onto a plate and keep warm in the oven while you make the remaining quesadillas. When ready to serve, cut the quesadillas into wedges, using a sharp knife or pizza cutter, and serve warm.

*adzuki beans* are one of the highest-protein and lowest-fat varieties of bean. They're also rich in soluble fibre, which helps digestion. Traditional Chinese medicine claims that adzuki beans benefit the bladder and kidneys, too.

# spinach bake

This is a recipe I have really perfected over the years. We love the browned cheese and the toasty pine nuts.

**SERVES:**
2 adults and
2 children

**PREPARATION TIME:**
20 minutes, plus at least 7 hours soaking

**COOKING TIME:**
1 hour 20 minutes

**STORAGE:**
Refrigerate for up to 3 days. Reheat until hot.

175g/6oz/1 cup brown basmati rice
1 tbsp kefir or natural yogurt
500ml/17fl oz/2 cups vegetable stock
55g/2oz/⅓ cup pine nuts
butter, for greasing
1 tbsp olive oil
1 large onion, finely chopped
4 eggs
225g/8oz frozen spinach, chopped
175g/6oz mature Cheddar cheese, grated
1 tbsp gluten-free vegetarian Worcestershire sauce
1 tsp dried thyme
1 tsp dried rosemary

**1** Put the rice, kefir and 500ml/17fl oz/2 cups warm water in a medium saucepan and leave to soak, covered, for 7 hours or overnight.

**2** Drain the rice, then return it to the pan and add the vegetable stock. Bring to the boil over a high heat, stir, then cover and reduce the heat to low. Simmer for 30 minutes until the rice is cooked.

**3** Meanwhile, preheat the grill to medium. Put the pine nuts on a baking sheet and grill for 2–3 minutes until lightly browned, checking frequently to ensure they don't burn. Set aside.

**4** Preheat the oven to 200°C/400°F/Gas 6 and grease a 20 x 20cm/ 8 x 8in baking dish with butter. Heat the oil in a frying pan, add the onion and cook over a medium heat for 3–4 minutes, stirring occasionally, until translucent. Remove from the heat.

**5** Put the eggs and spinach in a blender and blend for 1–2 minutes until smooth, then transfer to a large bowl.

**6** Add the pine nuts, onion, Cheddar, Worcestershire sauce, thyme and rosemary to the spinach mixture and mix well. Stir in the rice, then spoon the mixture into the baking dish.

**7** Bake for 45 minutes until lightly browned. Leave to cool for 5 minutes, then serve.

*spinach* is a nutritional star. It's rich in antioxidants, which support your child's immune system, and it's loaded with vitamins and minerals, including vitamins A and C and magnesium.

# kamut pasta with veggies & walnuts

SERVES:
2 adults and
2 children

PREPARATION
TIME:
30 minutes

COOKING TIME:
25 minutes

STORAGE:
Not suitable
for storage.

Toasting the walnuts makes all the difference in flavour in this delicious pasta that my children love.

½ tsp salt, plus extra for cooking the pasta
280g/10oz broccoli, cut into bite-sized florets
100g/3½oz/1 cup walnut halves, chopped
250g/9oz/3 cups dried Kamut pasta
135ml/4½fl oz/½ cup plus 2 tsp olive oil
1 onion, chopped
3 garlic cloves, chopped
10 basil leaves, torn
½ tsp salt

1 Preheat the grill to medium and bring a large pan of salted water to the boil. Put the broccoli in a steamer and steam, covered, over boiling water for 5 minutes until just soft. Meanwhile, put the walnuts on a small baking tray and grill for 4–5 minutes until just beginning to brown. Remove from the heat and leave to cool.

2 Cook the pasta according to the packet instructions. Meanwhile, heat a medium frying pan over a medium heat and add 2 teaspoons of the olive oil. When the oil is hot, add the onion and cook, stirring, for 8 minutes until lightly browned, then add the garlic and continue cooking for a further 2 minutes.

3 When the pasta has finished cooking, drain it and transfer to a large bowl. Add the onion mixture, broccoli, walnuts, basil, salt and remaining olive oil and mix well. Serve warm.

# lemon mackerel mayo & cucumber sandwiches

SERVES:
1 adult and 1 child

PREPARATION
TIME:
10 minutes

STORAGE:
Refrigerate the mackerel mixture for up to 3 days.

This is great for lunch – or lunchboxes when your child is older. The lemon juice adds freshness to the oily fish and the cucumber adds crunch.

125g/4¼oz smoked mackerel
2 tbsp mayonnaise, plus extra for spreading
3 tsp lemon juice
4 slices of wholemeal wheat bread
8 cucumber rounds

1 Remove and discard the skin from the mackerel and remove any bones, feeling the flesh with your fingers. Shred the mackerel into a small bowl with a fork. Add the mayonnaise and lemon juice and mix well.

2 Spread each slice of bread with a little mayonnaise. Put the cucumber rounds on two slices of the bread and spread the mackerel on top of them. Cover with the remaining slices of bread, cut each sandwich diagonally into two triangles and serve.

# arame rice with toasted seeds

Seaweed is the perfect way to add not only extra flavour but extra goodness, too. Toasted seeds make any dish more interesting because their roasted flavour is so good.

**SERVES:**
2 adults and
2 children

**PREPARATION TIME:**
10 minutes,
plus overnight
soaking

**COOKING TIME:**
30 minutes

**STORAGE:**
Refrigerate for
up to 1 day.
Reheat until hot.

175g/6oz/1 cup brown
   basmati rice
1 tbsp kefir or natural
   yogurt
5g/⅛oz/⅛ cup arame
2 tbsp sunflower seeds,
   pulsed in a blender
2 tbsp pumpkin seeds,
   pulsed in a blender
1 tsp tamari soy sauce
4 tbsp olive oil

**1** Put the rice, kefir and 500ml/17fl oz/2 cups warm water in a medium saucepan and leave to soak, covered, for 7 hours or overnight.

**2** Bring the rice to the boil over a high heat, reduce the heat to low and cook, covered, for 30 minutes until the rice is just tender.

**3** Meanwhile, crumble the arame into a bowl, using your hands or a pestle and mortar, and cover with boiled water. Leave to soak for 15 minutes, then drain.

**4** While the rice is cooking, heat a medium frying pan over a medium heat. When it is hot, add the sunflower and pumpkin seeds and the tamari and cook for 3–4 minutes, stirring with a wooden spoon, until lightly toasted and dry.

**5** Transfer the seeds to a medium serving bowl and add the rice, arame and olive oil. Mix well and serve warm or at room temperature.

*seaweeds*
are low in calories and
rich in essential minerals,
vitamins and protein. They
are also rich in very important
trace elements that are often
missing from conventional
land vegetables because of
the depletion of minerals
from the soil.

# tuna pie

The pie is so simple, and the combination of flavours is perfect. Wholemeal pastry is a must – the one used here is nutritious and easy to handle. Make sure to always buy sustainably sourced tuna (see page 40).

**SERVES:**
2 adults and
2 children

**PREPARATION TIME:**
50 minutes, plus
30 minutes chilling

**COOKING TIME:**
45 minutes

**STORAGE:**
Refrigerate the pastry for up to 3 days or freeze for up to 3 months. If you are not going to use the pastry the day you make it, mix in 1 tablespoon natural yogurt when you add the cold water. The baked pie is best eaten straightaway.

**_tuna_**
is an excellent source of omega-3 essential fatty acids, protein and many important minerals. Both fresh and tinned tuna are delicious, but many varieties of tuna are severely overfished, so make always read labels and buy sustainably sourced tuna.

120g/4¼oz/1 cup wholemeal spelt flour, plus extra for rolling
¾ tsp salt
85g/3oz butter, cut into pieces
4 tbsp tomato purée
90g/3¼oz tinned tuna in water or oil, drained
1 large tomato, sliced
1 tsp dried basil
1 tsp dried oregano
125g/4½oz buffalo mozzarella cheese, drained and sliced
125g/4½oz/1 cup pitted Kalamata olives, sliced into rings

**1** Put the flour and ½ teaspoon of the salt in a medium bowl and mix well. Using a pastry cutter, cut in the butter until the particles are the size of small peas. If you don't have a pastry cutter, rub the butter into the flour using your fingers. Add 3 tablespoons cold water and toss the mixture with a fork until the pastry is moist enough to hold together. Shape into a short log, wrap in cling film and refrigerate for 30 minutes.

**2** Preheat the oven to 200°C/400°F/Gas 6. Cut off about one-third of the pastry from the log, rewrap and set aside. Lightly sprinkle a large piece of baking parchment with flour and, using a rolling pin, roll out the larger piece of pastry to about 30cm/12in in diameter. Hold a 23cm/9in pie plate over the pastry to estimate the size. Lift the parchment paper and turn it over to drop the dough into the pie plate, then press the dough in to fit and press out any air pockets. Lightly sprinkle a new piece of baking parchment with flour and roll the remaining pastry into a 30cm/12in-wide circle and set aside.

**3** Spread the tomato purée over the bottom of the pastry to coat. Cover with half of the tuna, followed by half of the tomato slices, half of the basil and oregano, half of the mozzarella and half of the olives. Sprinkle with half of the remaining salt, then continue layering, starting with the remaining tomato slices, basil, oregano, mozzarella, olives and salt and ending with the remaining tuna.

**4** Cover the top of the pie with the remaining pastry. Fold the edges of the bottom crust over the edges of the top crust and press together with your fingers to flute. Carefully cut a 'T' into the middle of the top crust with a sharp knife to allow air to circulate during baking.

**5** Bake for 45 minutes until the crust is lightly browned and the pie is bubbling in the middle. Cut and serve hot.

# forks & knives

Now that your child is feeding herself and eating with the rest of the family, you can cook foods that are more sophisticated and require more coordination to eat. She'll have fun assembling Make-Your-Own Sushi and digging into the grown-up flavours found in dishes such as Prawn Pasta Bake and Curry Rice with Cranberries & Almonds. Let her help with easy tasks in the kitchen, too. This can be great fun and can spark a deeper interest in food. She may be little, but there's usually something to be poured, added or stirred that even little hands can manage – and when a child helps to make something, she usually really wants to eat it when it's ready. She can also just sit and watch while you explain what you're doing. It's a great way to spend time together and for her to learn.

*Blueberry Loaf (see page 135)*

# 2 to 3 years

Your child's digestive tract is now mature, so she can eat anything you can. Remember, though, that it's normal for a child's appetite to change. She'll be hungrier as she heads towards growth spurts, less so when she is tired or getting sick. Don't worry if she doesn't seem to be eating as much as you think she should. Always serve meals and encourage her to eat and then ensure she's getting healthy snacks as well. Some children are more into grazing, especially when they are little. If you write down what she actually eats during a day, you'd probably be surprised at how much it is.

**DEALING WITH A FUSSY CHILD:** Whereas your baby was compliant and would try anything, your toddler may like to argue with you about all sorts of things now and may not be so willing to try new foods. A great gift you can give her is to try foods with an open mind. If she says, 'I don't like that,' when she sees something new, explain that it might become her most favourite food in the entire world, but she won't know unless she tries it. Make it a game. Ask her to try something with her eyes closed. Can she guess what it is? If you can, take her food shopping and let her choose something new to try a few times a month. If she chooses something you've never had before, then you can learn together how to cook and eat it. There should be no pressure to eat something new, only encouragement or excitement – or reverse psychology: 'You don't want to try that!' or 'That's so yummy, I'm saving it for me and Daddy.' Whatever works with your child. Don't assume she won't like something just because she is little, either – she might surprise you. From when they were quite young, my kids loved things like roasted artichoke hearts, grilled garlic and caper berries.

If she starts to get fussy about eating vegetables, there are some great ways to encourage and get her engaged with her food. Try offering a bowl of vegetables cut into bite-sized pieces with olives, peas or sweetcorn to be eaten with a cocktail stick. Or mix the vegetables with mayonnaise, tzatziki, yogurt or a little olive oil and balsamic vinegar and a light sprinkle of salt. You could also offer a bowl of vegetables with a bowl of oil, tahini, hummus, mayonnaise, tzatziki or yogurt for dipping. When she is starving and can't possibly wait while you cook supper, put the veggies on the table first.

**HELPING IN THE KITCHEN:** Getting your child involved in the kitchen is another way to encourage her interest in food. Make the Baked Artichoke Hearts and let her cut the soft artichokes in half with a blunt knife. Teach her how to whisk an egg for the Potato & Parsnip Pancakes. Let her arrange the almonds for the Curry Rice on the baking tray and then taste how different they are raw versus after they're roasted and have cooled down.

## WONDERFOODS TO INCLUDE REGULARLY IN YOUR CHILD'S MEALS

*The foods listed here are nutritional powerhouses. Include them in your child's diet as often as you can.*

| FOOD | MAIN NUTRIENTS | BENEFITS TO CHILDREN | INTRODUCE THIS FOOD AT ... | RECIPES CONTAINING THIS FOOD |
|---|---|---|---|---|
| apples | Vitamin C, pectin, malic and tartaric acid | Detoxifier | 4–6 months | Apple Purée (see page 26) Rice & Mango Breakfast (see page 42) |
| almonds | Vitamin E, potassium and magnesium; high in monounsaturated fat | Aids absorption of calcium | 15–24 months | Curry Rice with Cranberries & Almonds (see page 121) |
| avocado | Oleic acid, potassium, folate, lutein, vitamin E | Anti-cancer | 4–6 months | Avocado Mash (see page 28) Guacamole (see page 144) |
| broccoli | Indols, carotenoids, iron | Anti-cancer | 4–6 months | Saucy Steam-Fry (see page 62) Roasted Veggies with Feta (see page 95) |
| oily fish | Omega-3 fats, EPA and protein | Builds brain and nerve tissue | 6–9 months | Salmon & Peas (see page 48) Tuna Pie (see page 107) |
| pumpkin and squash | Antioxidants, including beta-carotene and the rest of the carotenoids | Protect against infection | 4–6 months | Broad Bean & Pumpkin Purée (see page 45) Squash & Potato Soup (see page 80) |
| seeds | Omega-6 fats and omega-3 fats, zinc, magnesium and calcium | Anti-cancer; reduces risk of allergies and eczema | oil, from 4–6 months ground or chopped, from 15–24 months | Muesli Cookies (see page 133) Sesame & Raisin Bread Balls (see page 153) |
| seaweeds | Vitamin K, iodine, chlorophyll and alginic acid | Aids good thyroid function; detoxifier | 4–6 months for cooking beans 15–24 months, for direct feeding | Arame Rice with Toasted Seeds (see page 105) Make-Your-Own Sushi (see page 122) |
| sprouted beans and sprouted seeds | Enzymes | Improves digestion | 9–12 months | Brown Rice & Sprouts (see page 65) Toasted Quinoa & Vegetable Salad (see page 126) |
| whole grains | Fibre, B vitamins, iron, magnesium and selenium | Aids regular bowel function | 4–6 months | Cornbread Pudding (see page 79) Chicken with Apricot & Fennel Wild Rice (see page 130) |
| live, natural yogurt | Healthy bacteria; protein; calcium; phosphorus; vitamins B2, B12, B5; zinc | Strengthens immune system | 4–6 months, for soaking grains 9–12 months, for direct feeding | Mangetout, Cucumber & Yogurt Salad (see page 67) Prawn Pasta (see page 129) |

For other dishes, she can pour ingredients in or mix them. She'll love being with you – and she'll love helping.

**OPTIMIZING NUTRITION:** The chart on page 111 will help you to remember the wonderfoods that should form a regular part of your child's diet, if they don't already. We're all so busy that it's easy to fall back on old habits or cook the same thing again and again. We all do it. This list and the charts in this book will help to steer you back on track when you get in a rut. Sometimes life is so hectic that everything gets simplified. When that happens, you might find it hard to think, so just glance at the chart and remember that it doesn't take much time to sprinkle hemp seeds on cereal, mix vegetables with yogurt or add chopped sprouts to a pasta dish. When things ease up and you have a little more time again, make the dishes that require a bit more time.

**AVOIDING SWEETS:** Above all, don't be tempted to give your child junk food or sweets 'just so she eats something'. It's actually better that she doesn't eat because then she'll eat whatever you give her when she is hungry. It's just not worth creating bad habits. If she hasn't eaten lunch and then asks for a chocolate bar in the afternoon, don't give in. If you do, she'll ask for it all the time. Sometimes you can avoid the argument or distract her by ignoring her request and cutting up an apple or other fruit she likes and putting in on the table without saying anything. I like to have a bowl of fruit, nuts and healthy snacks such as wholemeal pretzels, crispbreads or brown rice crackers on the table or the counter where children can see it. This way, they can help themselves.

I don't offer a lot of desserts. I certainly don't have desserts after every meal or every day. There's no reason to have something sweet twice a day. It sets up a habit that can be very difficult to reverse. When there is no dessert at the end of a meal, kids are less likely to refuse to eat just because they know a more appealing dessert is coming.

**BROWN RICE MALT:** When I do bake, I always try to reduce the amount of sugar. With some baked goods, like banana bread, you can almost do without sugar entirely. It's also better to use brown rice malt than granulated sugar or even maple syrup, which are simple carbohydrates and cause a rush of energy followed by the sugar blues. Brown rice malt contains about 30 per cent soluble complex carbohydrates, 45 per cent maltose (grain-malt sugar) and only 3–4 per cent glucose (and 20 per cent water). Although the glucose hits the bloodstream almost immediately, the maltose takes up to 1½ hours to digest, while the complex carbs are digested and released for up to 4 hours, so the overall effect on blood sugar levels is much gentler than with simple sugars. If you want to convert old recipes that you have or new recipes you would like to try, for every 200g/¾oz/1 cup of sugar, use 185ml/6fl oz/¾ cup of brown rice malt and reduce liquids by 60ml/2fl oz/¼ cup.

There are a few recipes for sweet baked goods in this chapter. They're nice to have occasionally in the afternoons or on the weekends when everyone likes something special.

## MEAL PLANNER FOR CHILDREN AT 2–3 YEARS

*Here's an idea of how to work the recipes in this chapter into your child's diet. Just do your best, cook in batches when you can and always add nutrition.*

| DAY | BREAKFAST | MID-MORNING | LUNCH | MID-AFTERNOON | TEA |
|---|---|---|---|---|---|
| 1 | wholemeal rye toast with almond butter and yogurt | fruit (fresh or dried) | Prawn Pasta Bake (see page 129) steamed broccoli with 2 tsp seed oil raw carrot | Blueberry Loaf (see page 135) | Pecan & Stilton Stuffed Mushrooms (see page 118) rocket and sprouts salad |
| 2 | overnight porridge with soaked dried fruit | fruit (fresh or dried) | Hot Sardine Toasts (see page 128) steamed cauliflower raw peas | oatcakes with tahini | Chicken with Apricot & Fennel Wild Rice (see page 130) with 2 tsp seed oil avocado |
| 3 | Potato & Parsnip Pancakes (see page 116) | fruit (fresh or dried) | Baked Mushroom Open Sandwich with Tomato Sauce (see page 117) apple slices | Date, Oat & Hazelnut Bars (see page 134) | Haddock with Capers (see page 128) celery sticks steamed carrots with 2 tsp seed oil |
| 4 | Fruit Ambrosia (see page 60) sprouted bread | fruit (fresh or dried) | Potato Egg Mayonnaise (see page 125) cucumber sticks nori squares | hummus (see page 97) with 2 tsp seed oil wholemeal grissini | Pork with Gherkins (see page 131) mangetout sweet potato mash (see Carrot Purée on page 29) |
| 5 | scrambled eggs with Irish soda bread toast | fruit (fresh or dried) | Noodles with Vegetables (see page 125) | mixed nuts and seeds | Chilli Non Carne (see page 114) with grated cheese and tortillas spinach leaf salad and hemp seeds |
| 6 | Cornbread Pudding (see page 79) cottage cheese | fruit (fresh or dried) | Toasted Quinoa & Vegetable Salad (see page 126) sardines | Muesli Cookies (see page 133) | Make-Your-Own Sushi (see page 122) Baked Artichoke Hearts (see page 115) |
| 7 | Spelt French Toast (see page 79) | fruit (fresh or dried) | Curry Rice with Cranberries & Almonds (see page 121) grilled parsnip | rye crackers with goat's cheese | Brussels Sprouts & Barley Stew (see page 116) beetroot and yogurt salad with 2 tsp seed oil |

# chilli non carne

My husband Brian's favourite, this hearty chilli features weekly on my meal planner. If your children don't like spicy foods, reduce the chilli powder to ¼ teaspoon. If you want to make a meat chilli, use beef instead of the tempeh. Brown 175g/6oz/1 cup beef mince in 2 tablespoons olive oil and add it to the chilli 20 minutes before the chilli has finished cooking.

**SERVES:**
2 adults and
2 children

**PREPARATION TIME:**
25 minutes, plus overnight soaking

**COOKING TIME:**
2 hours 40 minutes

**STORAGE:**
Refrigerate the vegetarian chilli for up to 3 days and the beef chilli for up to 2 days.

125g/4½oz/¾ cup dried pinto beans
2 tsp lemon juice
1 strip of kombu, about 15 x 5cm/6 x 2in
1 tbsp olive oil
1 large onion, chopped
2 garlic cloves, crushed
175g/6oz tempeh, cut into small cubes
1 orange pepper, deseeded and chopped
480g/1lb 1oz/3⅓ cups chopped tinned tomatoes
½ tsp chilli powder
¾ tsp salt
175g/6oz mature Cheddar cheese, grated
200g/7oz low-salt corn chips (optional)

1 Put the beans and lemon juice in a medium saucepan, cover with warm water and leave to soak, covered, overnight.

2 Drain and rinse the beans. Return them to the pan and add 570ml/ 20fl oz/scant 2⅓ cups water. Bring to the boil over a high heat and boil for 10 minutes, skimming any scum that rises to the surface. Reduce the heat to low, add the kombu and cook, covered, for 2 hours until soft.

3 Meanwhile, heat a large saucepan over a medium-low heat and add the olive oil. When the oil is hot, add the onion and cook for 8 minutes, stirring continuously, until lightly browned. Add the garlic and cook, stirring, for a further 2 minutes. Stir in the tempeh, orange pepper, tomatoes and chilli powder.

4 Mash together the beans, kombu and cooking liquid and add to the tempeh mixture. Cook, covered, for 1 hour, stirring occasionally, until well cooked and the flavours have come together.

5 Stir in the salt and sprinkle the chilli generously with the Cheddar. Serve by itself or with the corn chips if desired.

*tempeh* is a naturally fermented soya food. It contains vitamin B12, which is vital for brain and nerve health, as well as probiotic bacteria, which support good digestive health.

# ▼ baked artichoke hearts

We love artichokes any which way, but combining them with crunchy roasted garlic and zingy lemon zest makes this beautiful dish divine. Jessie can eat almost half of this dish all by herself!

**SERVES:**
2 adults and
2 children

**PREPARATION TIME:**
15 minutes

**COOKING TIME:**
30 minutes

**STORAGE:**
Refrigerate for
up to 3 days.

**8 tbsp olive oil, plus extra for greasing**
**1 slice of wholemeal wheat bread or 30g/1oz/½ cup breadcrumbs**
**50g/1¾oz/½ cup grated Parmesan cheese**
**4 garlic cloves, finely chopped**
**1 tbsp chopped parsley**
**950g/2lb 2oz tinned artichoke hearts in water, drained, squeezed and halved lengthways**
**juice and zest of ½ lemon**

**1** Preheat the oven to 180°C/350°F/Gas 4 and grease a 23cm/9in round baking dish with olive oil. If using fresh bread, lightly toast it and then put it in a blender. Blend for 1 minute until breadcrumbs form. Put the breadcrumbs in a small bowl and mix in the olive oil, Parmesan, garlic, parsley and lemon juice and zest.

**2** Top each artichoke half with 1 teaspoon of the breadcrumb mixture and put the artichokes mixture-side up in the baking dish.

**3** Sprinkle any remaining breadcrumb mixture in the baking dish and bake for 30 minutes until golden brown. Serve hot.

# brussels sprouts & barley stew

If your child has only had Brussels sprouts with butter, she must try them like this. She'll find this rich, well-flavoured stew hearty and satisfying.

**SERVES:**
4 adults and
4 children

**PREPARATION TIME:**
30 minutes, plus at least 7 hours soaking

**COOKING TIME:**
1 hour 40 minutes

**STORAGE:**
Refrigerate for up to 3 days or freeze for up to 3 months.

185g/6½oz/1 cup pearl barley
1 tbsp kefir or natural yogurt
1 tbsp olive oil
1 large onion, chopped
4 tomatoes, halved
350g/12oz Brussels sprouts, trimmed and quartered lengthways
3 tbsp tamari
1 tbsp vegetarian Worcestershire sauce

**1** Put the barley and kefir in a large bowl, cover with warm water and leave to soak, covered, for 7 hours or overnight, then drain.

**2** Put the barley and 1.4l/48fl oz/5½ cups water in a very large saucepan and bring to the boil over a high heat. Reduce the heat to low and simmer, covered, for 45 minutes.

**3** Heat the olive oil in a small saucepan over a medium-high heat. Add the onion and cook for 10 minutes, stirring occasionally, until soft and slightly browned. Make a small triangular cut at the stem-end of each tomato half to remove the hard part, then chop the tomatoes.

**4** Add the onion, tomatoes, Brussels sprouts, tamari and Worcestershire sauce to the barley and simmer, covered, for a further 45 minutes until the barley is soft. Serve hot.

# potato & parsnip pancakes

This twist on the classic potato pancake is a good way to incorporate parsnip into a new favourite for your little one.

**SERVES:**
2 adults and
2 children

**PREPARATION TIME:**
10 minutes

**COOKING TIME:**
18 minutes

**STORAGE:**
Not suitable for storage.

3 eggs
85g/3oz/1 cup grated parsnip
140g/5oz/1 cup grated potato
5 tbsp wholemeal spelt flour
30g/1oz butter

**1** Put the eggs in a medium bowl and whisk with a wire whisk, then mix in the parsnip, potato and flour until blended.

**2** Preheat the oven to 70°C/150°F/Gas ¼. Melt the butter in a large frying pan over a medium-low heat, then drop tablespoonfuls of the parsnip mixture into the pan, spacing them well apart and flattening to 1cm/½in thick. Fry for 3 minutes on each side until lightly browned and cooked through. Transfer to a plate and keep warm in the oven while you make the remaining pancakes. Serve warm.

*parsnips* are packed with healthy potassium, which helps to regulate salt in the body. They're also an excellent source of dietary fibre and the antioxidant vitamin C.

# baked mushroom open sandwich with tomato sauce

With crunchy bread and melting cheese, these excellently flavoured warm sandwiches make a fabulous meal – one of Jessie's favourites. This recipe makes more tomato sauce than you will need for the sandwiches, but it's great to have to hand for quick meals.

**SERVES:**
2 adults and 2 children

**PREPARATION TIME:**
30 minutes, plus at least 1 hour chilling

**COOKING TIME:**
1 hour 50 minutes

**STORAGE:**
Refrigerate the sauce for up to 3 days or freeze in portion-sized jars for up to 3 months. The sandwiches are not suitable for storage.

- 2 tbsp olive oil, plus 2 tsp for frying
- 1 small onion, finely chopped
- 115g/4oz button mushrooms, brushed clean and chopped
- 55g/2oz/½ cup black pitted olives, sliced into rounds
- 115g/4oz mature Cheddar cheese, grated
- 2 garlic cloves, chopped
- 1 tsp dried oregano
- 1 large wholemeal wheat bloomer, sliced in half lengthways

**TOMATO SAUCE**
- 2 tbsp olive oil
- 2 large onions, chopped
- 1 red pepper, deseeded and chopped
- 4 garlic cloves, chopped
- 3 bay leaves
- 2 tbsp chopped parsley
- ½ tsp dried thyme
- 1 tsp dried oregano
- 1 tsp dried basil
- ½ tsp salt
- 650g/1lb 7oz tomatoes, chopped
- 455ml/16fl oz/scant 2 cups passata
- 85g/3oz tomato purée

**1** To make the tomato sauce, heat a large saucepan over a medium-high heat. Add the oil and when it is hot, add the onions. Cook, stirring occasionally, for 10 minutes until brown. Add the pepper and cook, stirring, for a further 5 minutes, then stir in the remaining ingredients. Bring the mixture to the boil, then reduce the heat to low and simmer, covered, for 1 hour, stirring occasionally.

**2** When the sauce has finished cooking, heat 2 teaspoons of the olive oil in a small frying pan over a medium heat. Add the onion and cook, stirring occasionally, for 10 minutes until soft. Remove from the heat.

**3** Put the mushrooms, olives, Cheddar, garlic, olive oil and oregano in a medium bowl. Add the onion and 320ml/11fl oz/scant 1⅓ cups of the tomato sauce and toss well. Cover and chill for at least 1 hour.

**4** Preheat the oven to 180°C/350°F/Gas 4. Remove some of the bread from the centre of each piece of bread to create a shallow hollow, then put the bread crust-side down on a baking sheet. Spread each half generously with the mushroom sauce. Bake for 30 minutes until the cheese has melted, then slice and serve hot.

*olives*
are an excellent source of vitamin E, which helps protect cells from oxidation. Green olives are picked before they're completely ripe, while black olives are picked ripe. Both are inedible until cured in either brine or oil.

# pecan & stilton stuffed mushrooms

**SERVES:**
2 adults and
2 children

**PREPARATION TIME:**
15 minutes

**COOKING TIME:**
30 minutes

**STORAGE:**
Not suitable
for storage.

If your child likes stuffed mushrooms, she'll absolutely love these. Serve them with a big mixed salad and some fresh wholemeal bread for a deliciously satisfying meal.

6 large, flat field
  mushrooms (the larger
  and flatter, the better),
  brushed clean
30g/1oz butter
1 large onion, finely
  chopped
30g/1oz/¼ cup pecan
  halves, broken in half
  lengthways (check for
  shell fragments)
2 slices of wholemeal
  spelt bread
175g/6oz Stilton cheese,
  crumbled
1 egg, beaten
4 tbsp chopped parsley
1 lemon, cut into
  6 wedges

**1** Preheat the grill to medium. Carefully remove the stems from the mushrooms. Set the caps aside and finely chop the stems. Melt the butter in medium frying pan over a medium-high heat, add the mushroom stems and onion and cook for 10 minutes, stirring occasionally, until the onion is just soft.

**2** Meanwhile, put the pecans in a baking dish and grill for 2–3 minutes until lightly browned. Remove from the grill and set aside.

**3** Preheat the oven to 180°C/350°F/Gas 4. Lightly toast the bread and put it in a blender. Blend for 1 minute until breadcrumbs form, then stir the breadcrumbs, pecans, Stilton, egg and parsley into the onion mixture.

**4** Put the mushroom caps rounded-side down on a large baking sheet and spoon the stuffing onto each one, dividing it equally among the six mushrooms. Bake for 20 minutes until the mushrooms are cooked and sizzling and the filling is lightly browned. Squeeze the lemon wedges over the mushrooms, and serve.

*pecans*
are super-rich in
good-quality oil. Because
they have a higher oil content
than most other nuts, they
go rancid more quickly, so
look for pale nuts when
you're shopping – the
paler, the fresher.

# mediterranean wholewheat fusilli

The vegetables in this recipe are cooked until they are soft and soupy, which is ideal when you're introducing your child to aubergine.

**SERVES:**
2 adults and
2 children

**PREPARATION TIME:**
15 minutes, plus
1 hour resting

**COOKING TIME:**
35 minutes

**STORAGE:**
Refrigerate for
up to 3 days.

200g/7oz aubergine, peeled and cut into 1cm/½in cubes
1 tsp salt, plus extra for cooking the pasta
3 tbsp olive oil, plus extra for drizzling
1 large onion, chopped
200g/7oz courgettes, cut into 1cm/½in cubes
200g/7oz tomatoes, cut into 1cm/½in cubes
3 garlic cloves, crushed
185ml/6fl oz/¾ cup vegetable stock
300g/10½oz dried wholewheat fusilli (spiral pasta)
¼–½ tsp cayenne pepper (optional)

**1** Put the aubergine in a colander, sprinkle with the salt and leave to rest in the sink for 1 hour.

**2** Heat the olive oil in a large frying pan over a medium heat. Add the onion and cook for 5 minutes, stirring occasionally, until beginning to soften. Reduce the heat to medium-low and add the aubergine, courgettes, tomatoes, garlic and vegetable stock. Continue cooking, covered, at a gentle simmer for 30 minutes, stirring occasionally, until the vegetables are cooked.

**3** When the vegetables have almost finished cooking, bring a large pan of salted water to the boil and cook the pasta according to the packet instructions, then drain and return it to the pan.

**4** Drizzle the pasta with a little olive oil and toss well, then divide it into four bowls. Spoon several tablespoons of the vegetable mixture over each child portion. Mix the cayenne pepper, if using, into the remaining vegetables and spoon it over the adult portions. Serve immediately.

*onions*
contain quercetin and chromium, powerful compounds that maintain a good hormone balance and protect the immune system. They also carry natural prebiotic fibre that stimulate the growth and function of probiotics.

# curry rice with cranberries & almonds

SERVES:
2 adults and
2 children

PREPARATION
TIME:
10 minutes,
plus at least
7 hours
soaking

COOKING TIME:
30 minutes

STORAGE:
Refrigerate for
up to 1 day.
Reheat until hot.

Here's a way to introduce tart cranberries to your child in a savoury dish. It also includes almonds, one of the healthiest nuts, which provide protein and good-quality fat. Here, they're toasted to add a nutty crunchiness.

**175g/6oz/1 cup brown basmati rice**
**1 tbsp kefir or natural yogurt**
**40g/1½oz/⅓ cup dried cranberries**
**1 tbsp olive oil**
**1 small onion, finely chopped**
**75g/2½oz/½ cup whole almonds with skins**
**1 tbsp curry powder**
**⅛ tsp cayenne pepper, ground**

**1** Put the rice, kefir and 500ml/17fl oz/2 cups warm water in a medium saucepan and leave to soak, covered, for 7 hours or overnight.

**2** Bring the rice to the boil over a high heat, then reduce the heat to low and cook, covered, for 30 minutes until the rice is just tender.

**3** While the rice is cooking, put the cranberries in a small bowl, cover with 4 tablespoons warm water and leave to soak for 15 minutes, then drain.

**4** Meanwhile, preheat the grill to medium. Heat the olive oil in a small frying pan over a medium heat until hot. Add the onion and cook for 10 minutes, stirring occasionally, until soft.

**5** Put the almonds on a baking sheet and grill for 3 minutes until lightly browned.

**6** Put the rice, cranberries, onion, almonds, curry powder and cayenne pepper in a medium bowl and toss well. Serve warm.

*almonds*
are, gram for gram, the most nutritionally dense nut. They are high in vitamin E and their skins contain flavanoid antioxidants, which makes a great combination. Keep the skins on in order to give your child the best nutritional kick possible.

# make-your-own sushi

Cook the rice, chop the vegetables, put it all on the table and your job is done! Letting your kids assemble their own sushi rolls is a great way to get them involved with their food – and it makes them feel grown up.

SERVES:
2 adults and
2 children

PREPARATION
TIME:
15 minutes, plus
at least 7 hours
soaking

COOKING TIME:
30 minutes

STORAGE:
Refrigerate the rice
for up to 1 day.
Reheat until hot.

175g/6oz/1 cup brown
basmati rice
1 tbsp kefir or natural
yogurt
1 small piece horseradish
root, peeled and finely
grated, or 3–4 tbsp
bottled horseradish
sauce
3–4 tbsp mayonnaise,
plus extra as needed
(optional)
12 sheets of nori, cut in
half crossways
1 cucumber, cut into thin
matchsticks
2 carrots, cut into thin
matchsticks
1 avocado, halved, pitted
and peeled, then cut
into strips
100g/3½oz alfalfa sprouts
umeboshi paste
wasabi paste

**1** Put the rice, kefir and 500ml/17fl oz/2 cups warm water in a medium saucepan and leave to soak, covered, for 7 hours or overnight.

**2** Bring the rice to the boil over a high heat, reduce the heat to low and cook, covered, for 30 minutes until the rice is just tender.

**3** While the rice is cooking, divide the grated horseradish root, if using, into two small bowls and mix with the mayonnaise. For adults, use equal amounts of horseradish and mayonnaise; for children use 1 part horseradish to 3 parts mayonnaise. If using a bottled horseradish sauce, simply put the sauce in a small serving bowl. Put the sauce on the table.

**4** Set the other components of the sushi on the table: put the nori sheets on two plates and divide the cucumber, carrots and avocado onto two additional plates. Divide the sprouts into two small bowls and put the umeboshi paste and wasabi paste in separate ramekins or small bowls. Divide the rice into two serving bowls.

**5** Show everyone how to make their own sushi – and give the family chef a break – although a two-year-old may need some help. To assemble the sushi, put 1 piece of nori, shiny-side down, on a plate. Spread a very thin strip of the umeboshi and wasabi pastes along the bottom of the nori – both are very strong in flavour. Then spread some of the horseradish sauce over, followed by 2 tablespoons of the rice. Top with 1–3 strips of vegetables and some sprouts, then roll the sushi upwards to form a log. It may not be as tidy as in the picture at right, but it will still be delicious. Eat immediately.

*umeboshi*
**is a fermented
Japanese plum. Its
powerful acidity has an
alkalizing effect on the
body. It combats tiredness,
stimulates digestion
and promotes the
elimination of
toxins.**

# ◀ noodles with vegetables

SERVES:
2 adults and
2 children

PREPARATION
TIME:
15 minutes

COOKING TIME:
15 minutes

STORAGE:
Not suitable
for storage.

Miso, a fermented soya food, is one of the world's most medicinal foods. Keep some in the fridge and get in the habit of adding it to soups and sauces.

**300g/10½oz udon noodles**
**200g/7oz carrots, cut into 3cm/1½in-long matchsticks**
**200g/7oz courgettes, cut into 3cm/1½in-long matchsticks**
**4 tbsp mellow brown miso**
**3 tbsp tahini**
**2 tbsp brown rice vinegar**
**1 tbsp mirin**
**1 garlic clove, chopped**
**4 spring onions, thinly sliced, to serve**
**salt**

**1** Bring a large saucepan of salted water to the boil and cook the udon noodles according to the packet instructions, then drain.

**2** While the noodles are cooking, put the carrots in a steamer and steam, covered, over boiling water for 2 minutes. Add the courgettes to the carrots and steam for further 4 minutes until just soft.

**3** Put the miso and tahini in a small saucepan and stir over a low heat until smooth. Add 80ml/2½fl oz/⅓ cup water and stir until smooth. Add the brown rice vinegar, mirin and garlic and heat until warmed through.

**4** Divide the noodles into four bowls and divide the steamed vegetables over the noodles. Top each portion with about 4 tablespoons of the sauce. Sprinkle with the spring onions and serve hot.

# potato egg mayonnaise

SERVES:
8 as a side dish or
4 as a main dish

PREPARATION
TIME:
15 minutes

COOKING TIME:
15 minutes

STORAGE:
Refrigerate for
up to 2 days.

This fantastic potato salad, livened up by vinegar and crisp vegetables, is excellent freshly made and warm – or chilled and taken on a picnic.

**550g/1lb 4oz potatoes, unpeeled, cut into 2cm/¾in cubes**
**4 eggs, at room temperature**
**1 small onion, finely chopped**
**2 garlic cloves, finely chopped**
**1 red pepper, deseeded and chopped**
**2 celery sticks, chopped**
**125ml/4fl oz/½ cup mayonnaise**
**4 tbsp white wine vinegar**

**1** Put the potatoes in steamer and steam, covered, over boiling water for 15 minutes until just soft. Remove from the heat and leave to cool.

**2** Meanwhile, pierce the large end of each egg with a pin. Bring a medium saucepan of water to the boil, add the eggs and cook for 9 minutes. Remove from the heat, drain the water from the pan and refill with cold water to cover the eggs. Leave until cool enough to handle, then drain. Peel the eggs, then quarter them lengthways and slice into bite-sized chunks.

**3** Put the eggs in a large bowl and add the potatoes, onion, garlic, red pepper, celery, mayonnaise and vinegar and mix well. Serve at room temperature or chilled.

# toasted quinoa & vegetable salad

SERVES:
2 adults and
2 children

PREPARATION
TIME:
20 minutes

COOKING TIME:
35 minutes

STORAGE:
Refrigerate for
up to 3 days, but
don't reheat. Serve
cold or at room
temperature.

This colourful, nutrient-packed salad is perfect for kids – Cassie absolutely loves it – and it's incredibly versatile: you can use any combination of finely chopped vegetables to cater to your child's growing tastes.

**85g/3oz/½ cup quinoa**
**75g/2½oz broccoli florets,**
  **cut into tiny pieces**
**juice of ½ lemon**
**1 tbsp olive oil**
**1 tbsp tahini**
**1 carrot, grated**
**½ yellow pepper,**
  **deseeded and finely**
  **chopped**
**140g/5oz cucumber, finely**
  **chopped**
**4 small spring onions,**
  **thinly sliced**
**30g/1oz alfalfa sprouts**

**1** Put the quinoa in a sieve and rinse under cold running water, then drain well. Transfer to a medium saucepan and toast over a high heat for 5 minutes, stirring continuously, until any excess water has evaporated and the quinoa has browned slightly and begun to pop.

**2** Add 240ml/8fl oz/scant 1 cup water and bring to the boil over a high heat. Reduce the temperature to low and simmer, covered, for 30 minutes until tender. Remove from the heat and leave to cool.

**3** Shortly before the quinoa has finished cooking, put the broccoli in a steamer and steam, covered, over boiling water for 3 minutes until tender. Meanwhile, put the lemon juice, olive oil and tahini in a small bowl and mix well, then set aside.

**4** Transfer the broccoli to a medium bowl and add the quinoa, carrot, yellow pepper, cucumber, spring onions and alfalfa sprouts and toss together. When ready to serve, pour the dressing over the vegetables, mix well and serve.

*tahini*
is rich in essential oils
that support healthy brain
and nerve development. It has
lots of iron and B vitamins,
which contribute to healthy cell
growth, and it's a good source
of methionine, an amino
acid that keeps the liver
healthy.

# hot sardine toasts

I could eat plain sardines until the cows come home, but if I ever feel like a change, this is the dish I crave. The creamy sauce paired with the piquant gherkins and capers make this dish especially appealing to children.

SERVES:
2 adults and
2 children

PREPARATION
TIME:
10 minutes

COOKING TIME:
40 minutes

STORAGE:
Not suitable
for storage.

**30g/1oz butter**
**1 tbsp plain flour**
**125ml/4fl oz/½ cup milk**
**80ml/2½fl oz/⅓ cup mayonnaise**
**1 tbsp finely chopped pitted green olives**
**2 tbsp finely chopped gherkin**
**2 tbsp finely chopped onion**
**2 tsp small capers**
**½ tsp cider vinegar**
**6 slices of wholemeal wheat bread**
**350g/12oz tinned sardines, drained**

1 Put the butter in the top of a double boiler or in a medium bowl resting over a pan of boiling water. Stir in the flour, then add the milk and mayonnaise, stirring until smooth. Continue stirring continuously for a further 30 minutes until the mixture forms a thick sauce. Remove from the heat and mix in the olives, gherkin, onion, capers and vinegar.

2 Preheat the grill to medium. While the grill is heating, toast the bread in a toaster and put it on a baking sheet. Cover each slice of toast with the sardines. If the sardines are large, mash them onto the bread so that you have a layer of sardines. Spoon about 3 tablespoons of the sauce over the sardines and grill for 3–4 minutes until hot and the sauce is bubbling. Serve immediately.

# haddock with capers

Children love this easy and delicious baked fish. The pretty cherry tomatoes and little green capers will catch their interest. Let them squeeze their own lemon and they'll like it even more.

SERVES:
2 adults and
2 children

PREPARATION
TIME:
10 minutes

COOKING TIME:
20 minutes

STORAGE:
Refrigerate for
up to 1 day.

**olive oil, for greasing**
**400g/14oz skinned haddock fillet, cut into 4 pieces**
**4 tsp capers**
**4 cherry tomatoes, quartered lengthways**
**1 lemon, cut into 4 wedges**
**salt**

1 Preheat the oven to 150°C/300°F/Gas 2 and grease a medium baking dish with olive oil. Put the fish pieces in the dish, sprinkle lightly with salt and put 1 teaspoon of the capers and four pieces of tomato on each piece.

2 Bake for 20 minutes until the fish is white. Squeeze 1 lemon wedge over each piece of fish and serve hot.

*lemons* are an excellent source of vitamin C, which is vital for a strong immune system. When added to foods, fresh lemon juice lifts the flavour and adds zing.

# ▼ prawn pasta bake

I always use yogurt instead of cream when I can because it's so much healthier, especially for little ones.

**SERVES:**
2 adults and
2 children

**PREPARATION TIME:**
10 minutes

**COOKING TIME:**
40 minutes

**STORAGE:**
Refrigerate for up to 2 days.

¼ tsp salt, plus extra for cooking the pasta
250g/9oz/2 cups wholewheat pasta, such as elbows or shells
300g/10½oz raw peeled prawns, cut into bite-sized pieces
200ml/7fl oz/scant 1 cup natural yogurt
½ tsp dried herbes de Provence
2 tbsp chopped parsley

**1** Preheat the oven to 180°C/350°F/Gas 4 and bring a large saucepan of salted water to the boil. Cook the pasta for 2 minutes less than the packet instructions suggest, then remove from the heat, drain and return to the pan.

**2** Mix in the prawns, yogurt, herbes de Provence, parsley and salt and transfer the mixture to a deep baking dish about 18 x 18cm/7 x 7in. Bake for 30 minutes until the prawns are cooked and the pasta is heated through, then serve.

# ▼ chicken with apricot & fennel wild rice

Wild rice is not technically rice: it's an aquatic cereal grass native to North America. Delicious on its own, it also makes a great stuffing.

SERVES:
2 adults and
2 children

PREPARATION TIME:
15 minutes, plus at least 7 hours soaking

COOKING TIME:
40 minutes

STORAGE:
Refrigerate the rice and chicken for up to 1 day. Reheat the rice until hot.

125g/4½oz/¾ cup wild rice
1 tbsp kefir or natural yogurt
5 tbsp plus 2 tsp olive oil
4 chicken breast fillets, about 100g/3½oz each, cut into strips
6 apricots, pitted and cubed
55g/2oz fennel, finely chopped
½ tsp salt

**1** Put the rice, kefir and 500ml/17fl oz/2 cups warm water in a medium saucepan and soak, covered, for 7 hours or overnight.

**2** Bring to the boil over a high heat, then reduce the heat to low and simmer, covered, for 40 minutes until the rice is just soft. Shortly before the rice has finished cooking, heat 2 teaspoons of the olive oil in a medium frying pan over a medium heat until hot. Put the chicken in the pan and cook for 5 minutes on each side until lightly browned and cooked through.

**3** Transfer the rice to a serving bowl. Mix in the apricots, fennel, salt and remaining olive oil and serve warm with the chicken.

# pork with gherkins

We were all a bit sceptical when my mom first made this dish, and then we were surprised by how much we loved it – especially when it was reheated the next day.

SERVES:
2 adults and
2 children

PREPARATION TIME:
15 minutes,
plus overnight soaking

COOKING TIME:
1 hour 10 minutes

STORAGE:
Refrigerate for up to 2 days. Tastes even better the day after it is made.

175g/6oz/1 cup brown basmati rice
1 tbsp kefir or natural yogurt
4 pork chops, about 900g/2lb
45g/1½oz butter
1 large onion, chopped
80ml/2½fl oz/⅓ cup red wine vinegar
1 large tomato, cubed
2 tbsp tomato purée
1 tbsp chopped parsley
½ tsp dried thyme
½ tsp dried tarragon
2 tbsp Dijon mustard
85g/3oz/½ cup sliced gherkins
salt

**1** Put the rice, kefir and 500ml/17fl oz/2 cups warm water in a medium saucepan and leave to soak, covered, for 7 hours or overnight.

**2** Sprinkle the pork chops with salt. Melt 15g/½oz of the butter in a large, heavy frying pan over a medium-high heat, then add the pork chops and cook for 5 minutes on each side until brown. Remove from the heat and transfer the chops to a platter.

**3** Add the remaining 30g/1oz of butter to the frying pan and melt over a medium heat. Add the onion and cook for 5 minutes, stirring occasionally, until beginning to brown. Add half of the vinegar and simmer until most of it has evaporated. Stir in the tomato, tomato purée, parsley, thyme, tarragon and 240ml/8fl oz/scant 1 cup water, then return chops to the pan and simmer, covered, for 45 minutes until tender.

**4** Meanwhile, bring the rice to the boil over a high heat, then reduce the heat to low, cover and cook for 30 minutes until just tender. Remove from the heat and set aside.

**5** Add the mustard, gherkins and remaining vinegar to the chops and mix well. Cook, covered, for a further 10 minutes, then serve, spooning the sauce over the rice and cutting the chops into smaller pieces for the child portions.

*herbs & spices* bring flavour and health to our foods whether they are used fresh or dried. Depending on the type, herbs and spices can help to strengthen the immune system and fight infection. Many are anti-bacterial and anti-fungal, too.

# muesli cookies

My kids love these very nutritious, very delicious cookies. The sesame seeds add a lovely toasty flavour, while the raisins and apricots add a sweet chewiness.

MAKES:
About 80 cookies

PREPARATION
TIME:
30 minutes

COOKING TIME:
45 minutes

STORAGE:
Store in an airtight container at room temperature for up to 5 days.

250g/9oz butter, softened
240ml/8fl oz/scant 1 cup brown rice syrup
1 egg
1 tsp vanilla extract
300g/10½oz/2½ cups wholemeal spelt flour
½ tsp baking powder
115g/4oz/1 cup porridge oats
55g/2oz/½ cup quinoa flakes
50g/1¾oz/½ cup millet flakes
75g/2½oz/½ cup sunflower seeds
30g/1oz/¼ cup sesame seeds
115g/4oz/¾ cup raisins
115g/4oz/¾ cup unsulphured dried apricots, finely chopped
50g/2oz/½ cup chocolate chips (optional)

**1** Preheat the oven to 180°C/350°F/Gas 4. Put the butter, brown rice syrup, egg, vanilla extract and 125ml/4fl oz/½ cup water in a large bowl and beat, using an electric mixer on medium speed or by hand using a whisk or wooden spoon, for 10 minutes until creamy.

**2** In a medium bowl, mix together the flour, baking powder, porridge oats, quinoa flakes, millet flakes, sunflower seeds, sesame seeds, raisins, apricots and chocolate chips, if using. Add the dry mixture to the wet mixture and stir with a wooden spoon until blended.

**3** Working in batches, drop 20 teaspoonfuls of the mixture onto a baking sheet, spacing them 2cm/¾in apart. Bake for 11 minutes until lightly browned. Remove from the oven and, using a spatula, transfer the cookies to a wire rack and leave to cool. Serve warm or at room temperature.

*seeds*
are high in nutrients such as iron, vitamin E and essential fatty acids. They are the 'eggs' that hold everything necessary to nourish a new plant. We should eat these nutritional wonders regularly, not only as the occasional snack.

# date, oat & hazelnut bars

Moist, dense and filling, these bars are great for a mid-morning or afternoon snack when your child wants something sweet. They're also easy to take out and about, so you always have a healthy snack to hand.

**MAKES:**
9 bars

**PREPARATION TIME:**
15 minutes, plus 10 minutes soaking

**COOKING TIME:**
1 hour 5 minutes

**STORAGE:**
Store in an airtight container at room temperature for up to 2 days and then refrigerate for up to 3 days.

70g/2½ oz/½ cup hazelnuts
90g/3¼oz butter, melted, plus extra for greasing
165g/5¾oz/1½ cups porridge oats
75g/2½oz/½ cup chopped dried dates
60ml/2fl oz/¼ cup brown rice malt
1 egg, beaten
1 tsp vanilla extract
55g/2oz/½ cup wholemeal spelt flour
1 tsp cinnamon
½ tsp baking powder

**1** Heat the grill to medium. Put the hazelnuts on a small baking tray and grill for 3 minutes until beginning to brown. Remove from the heat and leave to cool.

**2** Preheat oven to 180°C/350°F/Gas 4 and grease a 20 x 20cm/8 x 8in baking tin with butter. Put the porridge oats and dates in a bowl, stir in 375ml/13fl oz/1½ cups warm water and leave to soak for 10 minutes. Meanwhile, put the cooled hazelnuts in a plastic bag and pound them with a rolling pin or bottle until crushed, then add them to the oats.

**3** Add the brown rice syrup, butter, egg and vanilla extract to the oats and mix well.

**4** In another bowl, mix together the flour, cinnamon and baking powder, then add it to the oat mixture and mix well, using a wooden spoon or rubber spatula.

**5** Pour the mixture into the baking tin, smoothing the top with the back of the spoon. Bake for 1 hour until lightly browned. Remove from the oven and leave to cool slightly, then cut into 9 squares. Serve warm or at room temperature.

*brown rice malt*

is a naturally malted whole-grain sweetener. The highest-quality sweetener available, it is made by a slow, natural enzymatic process in which the grains of brown rice are broken down to yield a thick, sweet, rich liquid.

# blueberry loaf

Blueberries are one of nature's wonderfoods and add nutrition to everything they're used in. Eat them raw, make a pie or bake with them. You can serve this teacake as a delicious breakfast, a great afternoon snack or a delightful dessert that children will adore.

MAKES:
1 loaf

PREPARATION
TIME:
20 minutes

COOKING TIME:
1 hour 5 minutes

STORAGE:
Store in an airtight container for up to 2 days and then refrigerate for up to 3 days.

125g/4½oz butter, softened, plus extra for greasing
120g/4¼oz/1 cup white spelt flour, plus extra for flouring
115g/4oz/½ cup sugar
2 eggs
120g/4¼oz/1 cup wholemeal spelt flour
1 tsp baking powder
125ml/4fl oz/½ cup rice milk
250g/9oz/2 cups blueberries

1 Preheat the oven to 180°C/350°F/Gas 4 and grease and flour a 23 x 13cm/9 x 4in loaf tin. Put the butter and sugar in a large bowl and beat, using an electric mixer, at medium speed for 10 minutes until light and fluffy. Add the eggs, one at a time, beating well after each one.

2 In a medium bowl, combine the flours and baking powder. Add half of the flour mixture to the butter mixture and beat at low speed until just mixed, then beat in the rice milk followed by the remaining flour, beating until just blended. Fold in the blueberries, using a rubber spatula, and spoon the mixture into the loaf tin.

3 Bake for 1 hour 5 minutes until lightly browned, cracked in the middle and just pulling away from the sides of the tin. A cocktail stick inserted into the centre should come out clean. Remove from the oven and leave to cool in the tin on a wire rack for 15 minutes, then run a knife along the sides of the tin and turn the loaf out onto the wire rack to cool completely. Serve warm or at room temperature.

*blueberries*
are packed with vitamin C and vitamin E, making them one of the most antioxidant-rich of all fruits and vegetables. They're great for healthy cell growth and for maintaining healthy cholesterol levels.

# independence days

It probably seems like all you did was blink, and your baby turned into a walking, talking, independent little person with aspirations and opinions of his own. If you've followed the advice in this book, he's also developed a love of good food, so carry on giving him nutritious meals whenever you can. He's experiencing more of the world on his own now and forming friendships – some of which may last a lifetime. Parties and picnics are a great chance for him to socialize with other kids and share food. From simple dishes like Guacamole and Chickpea Pancakes to indulgent treats such as Cream Cheese & Salmon Blinis and Spelt Cake, the choices are plentiful, and you don't have to spend weeks planning. The lunchbox ideas here will help to ensure that he eats well at school, too.

*Mini Pitta Pizzas (see page 154)*

# 4 to 5 years

Your child will now be spending more time away from you at other people's houses, playgroups, parties and school or nursery. This means he will experience other foods and ways of eating. Carry on with the good eating habits you've established at home. This book is not about eating perfectly; it's about creating good habits so that your child eats really well most of the time. Then you don't have to worry about the rest of the time.

The recipes here are for picnics, lunchboxes, and parties, and are organized in that order. Many of the picnic dishes are great for light lunches at home, and the cake is great for birthdays and other special occasions.

I hope that by now you're feeling confident about cooking and have realized that it isn't some mysterious art. You may think some of these recipes would be better with a little more or a little less of something. Start recreating some of your favourites by swapping vegetables, changing ingredient proportions or simply omitting an item you don't like. The recipes aren't fixed in stone, so make them your own ... well, except the ones passed down to me by my mom. Those, of course, are sacred, so don't mess with them.

## Picnics

I love picnics. If you've got a good supply of food and drink, you can stay outside for a long time. The recipes in this section are all easy to prepare and portable. Supplement them with jars of olives, gherkins, sun-dried tomatoes, grilled artichoke hearts and grilled garlic. Meat and veggie sausages can be cooked beforehand and served warm or at room temperature, so bring little pots of mustard and ketchup for dipping. For kids, you can add some raw cucumber coins and carrot sticks and a pack of grissini. A selection of cheeses, savoury biscuits, organic chocolate, a bottle each of water and wine, and a thermos of jasmine tea, are great additions to round off the perfect spread.

In addition to plates, cutlery and cups, you'll need a cheese board, a small sharp knife, a corkscrew, kitchen roll, rubbish bags, hand wipes, spare clothes, sweaters, sunscreen, homeopathic remedies for bug and bee stings, plasters, a blanket, a ball and some toys. Pray for sun, head somewhere pretty and have some fun!

## Lunchboxes

I think that lunches for school must be easy enough to make in the morning. Even with only one child, I don't think that you want to be preparing more food at the end of the day after you have cleaned up the kitchen for the last time and could spend some time with your partner or simply enjoy some down time. Every lunchbox menu here can be thrown together in about 20 minutes. You just need a few things you can defrost from the freezer the night before, like pesto or pasta sauce. To make life easier, I steam a batch of vegetables to last for a couple of days, so that I don't have to cook them for every meal – and I use these for making lunches in the morning.

Again, variety is the key. Many children don't want a lot of any one thing at lunch (not even a whole sandwich), so a wide selection of foods increases the chances that he'll eat a better, more balanced meal. Remember, you're not there to help and encourage him over lunch any more, so make his lunchbox something he'll look forward to each day.

## Parties

Your child will be going to parties and will be exposed to an amazing range of foods, some new and wonderful, and some absolute junk. I don't want to create issues around food, so I let my kids eat what they want at parties. I do, however, remind them that this is not how we eat at home or every day, and I ask them to notice how they feel. It's meaningless to tell a child that something is bad for him, especially if you say it repeatedly. Instead, teach him to notice how food makes him feel physically, especially his tummy or head. I talked to Jessie about this when she was a toddler, just before she put a very sweet chocolately thing in her mouth. She listened, ate it and then came back to me a few minutes later and said, 'Oh, I'm all dizzy and spinny' (because of the sugar and caffeine). Don't think all of your efforts are wasted once your child leaves the house, either. Even if kids do rebel at some point, after a while they usually go back to what they knew before.

The party menus on page 141 provides a nice combination of cold, warm and finger foods that are great for parties. Each menu includes a few very quick and easy dishes, as well as foods that can be made in advance, which makes planning and executing the food for the party easier. All of the recipes are packed with good, nutritious ingredients, and they also have a whimsical element so kids will find them fun to eat. Finger foods such as Mini Pitta Pizzas, Cream Cheese & Salmon Blinis and Cherry Tomatoes with Hummus & Capers, for example, are always popular.

Because I serve sweets and desserts so rarely, I like to do something really special for birthdays and festive occasions. The cake recipe on page 159 is especially great for kids. Not only does it taste delicious, but it also provides nutrition because about half of the flour is wholemeal spelt flour. If you decorate it with cut fruit, which can be quite pretty, you avoid a sugary icing, too. The cake is also easy to handle when you want to transfer it to a pretty serving plate or for cutting into interesting shapes. I've made it into everything from a spaceship to a fairy castle.

If you're planning a party for a four- or five-year old, six is the ideal number of guests – unless you want to invite the whole class. Allow two hours, usually 3:00 to 5:00 in the afternoon. Have someone who is close to your child there to help out. Start with some sort of art activity and have your helper run some games while you lay the table. Present each

## MEAL PLANNER: LUNCHBOXES

*A varied menu helps to liven up your child's lunch and keep him interested in his food. A small juice box makes a nice occasional treat in addition to water.*

| MONDAY | TUESDAY | WEDNESDAY | THURSDAY | FRIDAY |
|---|---|---|---|---|
| Cheddar & Watercress Sandwich (see page 149) | Spelt Pasta with Pesto (see page 148) | Lemon Mackerel Mayo & Cucumber Sandwiches (see page 104) | Corn Pasta with Tomato Sauce (see page 148) | Hemp Seed & Egg Mayo Sandwich (see page 150) |
| celery sticks and broccoli florets | Cucumber & Tomato Salad (see page 151) | Carrot & Pea Salad (see page 151) | Rocket & Lemon Salad (see page 150) | cauliflower florets and red pepper |
| blueberries | ½ apple, sliced and sprinkled with lemon juice | grapes | ½ banana (skin on) | unsulphured dried apricots |
| seeds and nori squares | yogurt | water | almonds | oatcakes |
| water | water | | water | water |

**For variety other weeks, try substituting some of the above with the following:**

| SUBSTITUTE ... | WITH ... |
|---|---|
| vegetables | asparagus, avocado (must be sprinkled with lemon), raw courgette rounds, fennel, green beans, mangetout, sugar snap peas, raw or cooked turnip rounds, swede and so on |
| unsulphured dried apricots | dried cranberries, dates, figs, dried mango, pineapple, prunes, raisins, sultanas and so on |
| oatcakes | corn cakes, rice cakes, rye crispbreads, Japanese brown rice crackers, wholemeal wheat or spelt grissini/pretzels and so on |
| fruit | other berries, clementines, kiwi, orange segments, satsumas and so on |
| almonds | Brazil nuts, hazelnuts, macadamia nuts, pecans, pine nuts, pistachio nuts and walnuts |

food on two plates, one at each end of the table, so that all the kids can easily reach everything. At 4:00, it's time to eat. After that, have the birthday star open presents with all of the children gathered around. Have your helper keep a list of who gave what in order to avoid confusion when writing thank-you notes. In the meantime, you can get the table ready for everyone's favourite moment: the cake. Around 4:30, it's time for singing, candles and cake. Afterwards, play another game or take everyone outside to play, if the weather allows, until the parents arrive to collect the children. You can also invite the parents to come a little earlier for cake and just cut it into smaller pieces.

## PARTY MENUS (FOR 8 CHILDREN)

*Although you can mix and match the ten party recipes in this chapter any way you like, the two menus below are ones that I often use.*

| MENU 1 | QUANTITY PER CHILD | PREPARATION TIME (IN MINUTES) | COOKING TIME (IN MINUTES) |
|---|---|---|---|
| Sesame & Raisin Bread Balls (see page 153) | 2 | 30 | 30 |
| Cherry Tomatoes with Hummus & Capers (see page 154) | 3–4 | 20 | – |
| Chickpea Pancakes (see page 152) | 1–2 | 10 | 10 |
| Cheesy Polenta Bites (see page 156) | 4 | 10 | 20 |
| Sweet Potato Fish Balls (see page 157) | 3 | 15 | 25 |
| Spelt Cake (see page 159) | | | |
| TOTAL | 13–15 | 85 | 75 |

| MENU 2 | QUANTITY PER CHILD | PREPARATION TIME (IN MINUTES) | COOKING TIME (IN MINUTES) |
|---|---|---|---|
| Cherry Tomatoes with Hummus & Capers (see page 154) | 3–4 | 20 | – |
| Cream Cheese & Salmon Blinis (see page 157) | 4–5 | 15 | 20 |
| Mini Pitta Pizzas (see page 154) | 1 | 10 | 5 |
| Sweet Potato & Carrot Patties (see page 155) | 1–2 | 15 | 35 |
| Tofu Squares (see page 156) | 3 | 10 | 5 |
| Spelt Cake (see page 159) | | | |
| TOTAL | 12–15 | 70 | 65 |

# wholemeal spelt bread

Making your own bread is so satisfying, and this dense, moist loaf is proof that it's also easy – and doesn't require a bread machine.

MAKES:
1 large loaf

PREPARATION TIME:
20 minutes, plus 3–48 hours rising

COOKING TIME:
30 minutes

STORAGE:
Store the baked bread in an airtight container for up to 4 days. The dough can be made to the end of step 1 and frozen (all or half) in an airtight plastic bag for up to 3 months. To bake, put the dough on a greased baking sheet, leave to come to room temperature and then rise for 1 hour. Then bake as in step 5.

*long fermentation*

**with kefir or yogurt allows the phytic acid, hard-to-digest proteins and complex starches in the flour to break down. This method also increases vitamin content and makes the nutrients in the grains more available for absorption.**

2 tsp olive oil, plus oil for greasing
660g/1lb 7½oz/5½ cups wholemeal spelt flour
1 tbsp active dried yeast
1 tbsp salt
1 tbsp kefir or natural yogurt
butter, for greasing

1 Grease a medium bowl with olive oil and set aside. In a large bowl, mix together the flour, yeast and salt. Add the olive oil, kefir and 375ml/13fl oz/1½ cups lukewarm water. Mix with your hands until it has nearly all come together, adding an additional 1–2 tablespoons water if necessary. Tip the contents of the bowl onto a work surface and knead by stretching the dough away from you, then gathering it back, turning it 90 degrees and repeating, working in all of the flour as you knead until it is incorporated. The dough may seem a little dry at first, but the ingredients will come together as you work it. Knead for 10 minutes until smooth and elastic. If the dough is sticking to your hands, add a little more flour a bit at a time; if it is too dry for the dry ingredients to come together, add a little more water.

2 Transfer the dough to the oiled bowl, rubbing a little olive oil over the surface of the dough. Put a clean, damp tea towel on the surface of the dough so that it doesn't dry out and form a crust, and chill for 24 hours. Alternatively, if you don't want to wait for a long fermentation and want to bake the loaf on the same day, leave the covered dough to rise at room temperature for 1½–2 hours until doubled in size, then skip step 3 and go directly to step 4.

3 Take the dough out of the fridge and knock it back thoroughly to get all of the air out. Turn it onto a work surface, knead for 1 minute, shape into a ball and put it back in the bowl. Cover again with the damp tea towel and put it back in the fridge for a further 24 hours.

4 Grease a baking sheet with butter and set aside. Turn the dough out onto a work surface and knock it back thoroughly. Knead for 1 minute, then shape it into a ball and put it on the baking sheet. Cover with the damp tea towel and leave to rise at room temperature for 1–1½ hours until doubled in size.

5 Preheat the oven to 220°C/425°F/Gas 7. Remove the tea towel and put the bread in the oven. Bake for 10 minutes, then reduce the oven temperature to 190°C/375°F/Gas 5 and bake for a further 20 minutes until the loaf is golden brown and sounds hollow when tapped. Remove from the oven and leave to cool on a wire rack for 15 minutes. Serve warm or at room temperature.

# adzuki yogurt dip

A few dips are always a good idea at a picnic, and this one is a nice change from hummus. It's mild, smooth and creamy – and a pretty pink colour.

**SERVES:**
8

**PREPARATION TIME:**
10 minutes, plus overnight soaking

**COOKING TIME:**
55 minutes

**STORAGE:**
Refrigerate for up to 2 days.

200g/7oz/1 cup dried adzuki beans
6 tsp lemon juice
1 strip of kombu, about 15 x 5cm/6 x 2in
125ml/4fl oz/½ cup Greek yogurt
1 tsp ground cumin
1 tsp salt
vegetable crudités (optional), to serve
tortilla chips (optional), to serve

**1** Put the beans and 2 teaspoons of the lemon juice in a medium saucepan, cover with warm water and leave to soak, covered, overnight.

**2** Drain and rinse the beans. Return them to the pan and add 750ml/26fl oz/3 cups water. Bring to the boil over a high heat and boil for 10 minutes, skimming any scum that rises to the surface. Reduce the heat to low, add the kombu and cook, covered, for 45 minutes until the beans are soft. The beans should remain covered with water, so add extra boiled water during cooking if necessary. Then drain and leave to cool.

**3** Put the beans and kombu, yogurt, cumin, salt and remaining lemon juice in a blender. Blend for 1 minute until smooth, then serve with vegetable crudités or tortilla chips.

# egg mayonnaise

This is the egg mayonnaise I grew up with – a wonderful variation of the classic recipe. It's a great dish for picnics because it's so portable. You can eat it by itself or spread it on savoury biscuits or bread.

**SERVES:**
8

**PREPARATION TIME:**
15 minutes

**COOKING TIME:**
9 minutes

**STORAGE:**
Refrigerate for up to 2 days.

6 eggs, at room temperature
2 large gherkins, cubed
1 small red onion, finely chopped
1 garlic clove, chopped
2 tbsp chopped parsley
⅛ tsp salt
2 tbsp mayonnaise
2 tbsp non-hot mustard

**1** Pierce the large end of each egg with a pin. Bring a medium saucepan of water to the boil and, using a spoon, carefully put the eggs in the water. Boil for 9 minutes, then remove from the heat, drain the hot water from the pan and refill it with cold water to cool the eggs and stop them cooking. Set aside until cool enough to handle.

**2** Peel the eggs, put them in a medium bowl and mash with a fork or potato masher. Add the gherkins, onion, garlic, parsley, salt, mayonnaise and mustard and mix well. Serve at room temperature or chilled.

# ▼ guacamole

I'm always surprised at how quickly two avocados disappear at a picnic when there's always so much other food. Jessie, especially, gives this winning recipe an enthusiastic thumbs up every time.

SERVES:
8

PREPARATION TIME:
15 minutes

STORAGE:
Refrigerate for up to 3 days.

**2 avocados, halved and pitted**
**1 tomato, finely chopped**
**juice of 1 lemon**
**¼ tsp salt**
**⅛ tsp Tabasco sauce**
**vegetable sticks (optional), to serve**

**1** Scoop the avocado flesh into a medium bowl and mash using a fork, leaving it a bit lumpy.

**2** Add the tomato, lemon juice, salt and Tabasco and mix well. Serve chilled or at room temperature.

# marinated cauliflower

This surprisingly simple and delicious way to serve cauliflower appeals to children and adults alike.

SERVES:
8

PREPARATION TIME:
10 minutes, plus 20 minutes marinating

COOKING TIME:
5 minutes

STORAGE:
Keep at room temperature in a covered bowl for up to 4 hours.

500g/1lb 2oz cauliflower, cut into bite-sized florets
4 tbsp olive oil
2 tbsp brown rice vinegar

**1** Put the cauliflower in a steamer and steam, covered, over boiling water for 5 minutes until just tender.

**2** Transfer the cauliflower to a medium serving bowl and, while it's still warm, drizzle over the olive oil and vinegar. Toss well and then leave to marinate at room temperature for at least 20 minutes while you pack your picnic things or travel to the picnic.
Serve at room temperature.

*brown rice vinegar* is treasured for its mellow flavour and light sweetness. The best kind is made in the traditional Japanese way, with only fermented sweet brown rice and water.

# parsley pesto penne

Pesto, with its toasty pine nuts, fresh herbs, pungent garlic and quality olive oil, is heaven with pasta. This recipe uses parsley instead of basil and is made without cheese.

SERVES:
8

PREPARATION TIME:
15 minutes

COOKING TIME:
10 minutes

STORAGE:
Refrigerate the pesto for up to 3 days or freeze for up to 3 months.

55g/2oz/⅓ cup pine nuts
¾ tsp salt, plus extra for cooking the pasta
450g/1lb/4 cups dried wholewheat penne pasta
85g/3oz/2 cups chopped parsley
3 garlic cloves, crushed
125ml/4fl oz/½ cup olive oil

**1** Preheat the grill to medium. Put the pine nuts on a baking sheet and grill for 1 minute until toasted, watching carefully so they do not burn. Remove from the grill and set aside.

**2** Bring a large saucepan of salted water to the boil. Add the pasta and cook according to the packet instructions, then drain and transfer to a large bowl.

**3** While the pasta is cooking, put the pine nuts, parsley, garlic, salt and olive oil in a blender and blend for 1 minute until smooth.

**4** Pour the pesto over the pasta and toss well. Serve warm.

# romaine salad with shiitake mushrooms & garlic ▶

This gorgeous, full-flavoured and sturdy salad is great for picnics. You can mix the dressing in a little jar and dress the salad when you're ready to eat.

1 romaine lettuce,
    washed and dried
30g/1oz butter
10–12 garlic cloves, cut
    lengthways into slivers
200g/7oz shiitake
    mushrooms, brushed
    clean, stems discarded,
    and caps cut into
    1cm/½in-thick slices
3 tbsp olive oil
1 tbsp balsamic vinegar
2 tbsp shaved Parmesan
    cheese
salt

**1** Reserve the smaller centre leaves from the lettuce and chop the remaining leaves in 1cm/½in wide strips. Put them in a large salad bowl and set aside.

**2** Heat a large frying pan over a medium-high heat. Add the butter and garlic and cook for 4 minutes, stirring occasionally, until starting to brown. Add the mushrooms and continue cooking for 10 minutes, stirring continuously, until brown and crisp. Remove from the heat and leave to cool.

**3** Add the mushroom mixture to the chopped lettuce and sprinkle with the olive oil, balsamic vinegar and Parmesan. Season with salt and toss well. Spoon the salad into the reserved lettuce leaves and serve.

# lemon–cinnamon apple slices

Fresh fruit is a must on a picnic, and these refreshing, ready-to-eat slices are great for little hands.

3 apples, halved, cored
    and cut into wedges
juice of ½ lemon
½ tsp cinnamon

**1** Put the apples in a medium bowl. Sprinkle with the lemon juice and toss until well coated.

**2** Sprinkle the cinnamon over the apples and toss until well coated. Serve either before or after the meal.

*cinnamon*
comes from the bark of the cinnamon tree and is one of the oldest known spices. A great source of manganese, iron and calcium, it's also a natural food preservative, inhibiting bacteria and preventing spoiling.

# spelt pasta with pesto

SERVES:
1

PREPARATION
TIME:
5 minutes

COOKING TIME:
10 minutes

Warm a thermos with boiling water before packing this easy dish, and by lunchtime your child will have delicious, still-warm pasta to savour.

40g/1½oz/½ cup dried
　wholemeal spelt penne
2 tbsp basil pesto
　(see page 154)
salt

**1** Bring a small saucepan of salted water to the boil over a high heat and cook the pasta according to the packet instructions. Meanwhile, fill a small thermos with boiling water and set aside.

**2** Drain the pasta, then return it to the pan and mix in the pesto.

**3** Drain the hot water from the thermos and transfer the pasta into the thermos. Don't forget to pack a fork!

# corn pasta with tomato sauce

SERVES:
1

PREPARATION
TIME:
5 minutes

COOKING TIME:
10 minutes

Corn pasta adds a different grain to your lunchbox rota. This dish is a great opportunity to use some of the homemade tomato sauce that you've been keeping in the freezer – simply defrost it in the fridge the night before or in a pan over a medium heat while the pasta cooks.

salt
40g/1½oz/¾ cup corn
　spirelli
2 tbsp tomato sauce
　(see page 117)

**1** Bring a small saucepan of salted water to the boil over a high heat and cook the pasta according to the packet instructions. Meanwhile, fill a thermos with boiling water and set aside.

**2** Drain the pasta, then return it to the pan. Add the tomato sauce and mix well.

**3** Drain the hot water from the thermos and transfer the pasta into the thermos.

# ▲ cheddar & watercress sandwich

Mature Cheddar is wonderfully flavourful. Nicholas loves it matched with the mustard, mayonnaise and watercress in this recipe.

**SERVES:**
1

**PREPARATION TIME:**
10 minutes

**1 slice of wholemeal wheat bread**
**non-hot mustard, for spreading**
**mayonnaise, for spreading**
**30g/1oz mature Cheddar cheese, sliced**
**2–3 watercress sprigs**

**1** If the bread is fresh, use it as is. If it is frozen, make the sandwich with frozen bread – it will thaw and be soft by the time your child has lunch. Cut the bread in half and spread one half with mustard and the other with mayo.

**2** Put the cheese on one half of the bread, top with the watercress and then cover with the other half of the bread.

**3** Wrap the sandwich in greaseproof paper, put it in a little plastic bag and seal to keep it fresh. Have your child bring the plastic bag back home so you can re-use it many times, washing it out as necessary.

# hemp seed & egg mayo sandwich

SERVES:
1

PREPARATION TIME:
10 minutes

COOKING TIME:
9 minutes

Hemp seeds have a subtle, nutty flavour, so your child may not even taste them – but they add excellent nutrition to a lovely sandwich.

**1 egg, at room temperature**
**1 tbsp mayonnaise, plus extra for spreading**
**1 tsp shelled hemp seeds**
**1 slice of wholemeal rye bread**

**1** Pierce the large end of the egg with a pin. Bring a small saucepan of water to the boil and, using a spoon, carefully put the eggs in the water. Boil for 9 minutes, then remove from the heat, drain the hot water from the pan and refill it with cold water to cool the egg and stop it cooking. Leave to cool for 5 minutes.

**2** Peel the egg and put it in a small bowl. Add the mayonnaise and mash with a fork. Add the hemp seeds and mix well.

**3** Cut the bread in half and spread with mayonnaise. Spoon the egg mayo onto one half of the bread (you will have some left over) and then cover with the other half of the bread. Wrap the sandwich in greaseproof paper and then put in a little plastic bag and seal to keep it fresh. Have your child bring the plastic bag back home so you can re-use it many times, washing it out as necessary.

# rocket & lemon salad

SERVES:
1

PREPARATION TIME:
5 minutes

Rocket with lemon juice is divine – and because you're not adding olive oil, the leaves are still fresh and crisp at lunchtime.

**1 handful rocket leaves, roughly chopped**
**1 lemon wedge**

**1** Put the rocket in a small container and squeeze the lemon over.

**2** Mix well and seal the container.

*rocket*
and other bitter salad greens are an excellent source of antioxidants. Rocket is also packed with vitamin C, which is important for healthy teeth and gums and for fighting infection; and calcium, which is needed for strong bones.

# carrot & pea salad

SERVES:
1

PREPARATION
TIME:
5 minutes

Jessie loves this colourful salad. It's lovely and fresh, and the balsamic vinegar gives it a gentle sweetness. The frozen peas will defrost by lunchtime and will really brighten up your child's meal.

**1 small carrot, grated**
**2 tbsp frozen peas**
**1 tsp balsamic vinegar**

**1** Put the carrot, peas (leave frozen) and vinegar in a bowl and mix well.

**2** Transfer to a small container and seal.

# cucumber & tomato salad

SERVES:
1

PREPARATION
TIME:
10 minutes

Crunchy and refreshing, this salad will liven up your child's lunchbox. Cucumber and tomato are a great duo, and the mayonnaise adds a delightful creaminess.

**5cm/2in piece cucumber,**
**quartered lengthways,**
**then quartered**
**crossways**
**4 cherry tomatoes,**
**quartered**
**1 tbsp mayonnaise**

**1** Put the cucumber, tomato and mayonnaise in a bowl and mix well.

**2** Transfer to a small container and seal.

*cucumber* packs a nutritional punch. Among other nutrients, it provides silica, which helps to strengthen connective tissue. It also has folate and vitamins A and C. Organic cucumbers have higher levels of vitamin C than conventional ones.

# chickpea pancakes

Finger foods are great at parties and these are perfect for little fingers. They have a nice flavour without being too strong.

MAKES:
12 pancakes

PREPARATION TIME:
10 minutes, plus overnight soaking

COOKING TIME:
2 hours 25 minutes

STORAGE:
Refrigerate the cooked pancakes for up to 3 days.

**115g/4oz/½ cup dried chickpeas**
**2 tsp lemon juice**
**1 strip of kombu, about 8 x 5cm/3¼ x 2in**
**wholemeal wheat or spelt flour, as needed (optional)**
**1 tsp ground cumin**
**½ tsp salt**

**1** Put the chickpeas and lemon juice in a medium saucepan, cover with warm water and leave to soak, covered, overnight.

**2** Drain and rinse the chickpeas. Return them to the pan and add 455ml/16fl oz/scant 2 cups water. Bring to the boil over a high heat and boil for 10 minutes, skimming any scum that rises to the surface. Add the kombu, reduce the heat to low and cook, covered, for 2 hours until tender. Remove from the heat and drain. If using a blender with a plastic container, leave the chickpeas and kombu to cool completely before blending.

**3** Transfer the chickpeas and kombu to a blender and blend for 1 minute until smooth, adding just enough fresh water to form a thick mixture. If you add too much water and the mixture is runny, add a little flour, 1 tablespoon at a time, until it thickens. Transfer the mixture to a bowl and stir in the cumin and salt.

**4** Heat a griddle over a medium heat. Working in batches if necessary, drop teaspoonfuls of the chickpea mixture onto the griddle. They will spread a little and should be about 3cm/1¼in in diameter. Cook for 2–3 minutes until bubbles pop through the surface and the underside of the pancake is lightly browned. Flip over and cook for a further 2–3 minutes until lightly browned. Serve hot or warm.

*chickpeas* are high in fibre, which helps to avoid rapid rises in blood sugar levels after eating. Combined with grains, they are a fat-free protein, so serve them with good oils, such as hemp seed or flaxseed oil, for a well-rounded, healthy meal.

# sesame & raisin bread balls

With their little sweet raisin bits inside, these are great for parties, especially warm from the oven. They also help fill up little tummies.

**MAKES:**
40–45 balls

**PREPARATION TIME:**
30 minutes, plus 3½ hours rising

**COOKING TIME:**
35 minutes

**STORAGE:**
Store the baked bread balls in an airtight container for up to 2 days. The dough can be made to the end of step 1 and refrigerated up to 3 days. Knock it back once a day and re-cover, or freeze for up to 3 months in a plastic bag, squeezing out any excess air. To bake, leave the dough to come to room temperature and double in size, then continue from step 3.

*raisins*
are excellent for relieving constipation and reducing acidity. They're antiviral and antibacterial, too. Raisins are packed with iron and aid bone and teeth health and vision.

1 tsp olive oil, plus extra for greasing and coating the dough
300g/10½oz/2½ cups wholemeal spelt flour
1½ tsp active dried yeast
1½ tsp salt
1½ tsp kefir or natural yogurt
butter, for greasing
2 tbsp sesame seeds
30g/1oz/¼ cup raisins, coarsely chopped

1 Grease a medium bowl with olive oil and set aside. In a large bowl, mix together the flour, yeast and salt. Add the olive oil, kefir and 185ml/6fl oz/¾ cup lukewarm water. Mix with your hands until it has nearly all come together, adding an additional 1–2 tablespoons water if necessary. Tip the contents of the bowl onto a work surface and knead by stretching the dough away from you, then gathering it back, turning it 90 degrees and repeating, working in all of the flour as you knead until it is incorporated. The dough may seem a little dry at first, but the ingredients will come together as you work it. Knead for 10 minutes until smooth and elastic. If the dough is sticking to your hands, add a little more flour a bit at a time; if it is too dry for the dry ingredients to come together, add a little more water.

2 Transfer the dough to the oiled bowl, rubbing a little olive oil over the surface of the dough. Put a clean, damp tea towel on the surface of the dough so that it doesn't dry out and form a crust, and leave to rise at room temperature for 1½–2 hours until doubled in size.

3 Grease a baking sheet with butter and set aside. Turn the dough out onto a work surface and knock back thoroughly. Knead for 1 minute, then shape it into a ball and transfer to the baking sheet. Cover with the damp tea towel and leave to rise at room temperature for 1–1½ hours until doubled in size.

4 Preheat the oven to 220°C/425°F/Gas 7. Put the sesame seeds in a shallow bowl and set aside. Punch down the dough again and flatten it with your hand, then pour the raisins on top and knead them into the dough for 1 minute or until incorporated. Pull off small pieces of the dough and roll them into 2.5cm/1in balls, pinching the dough around any raisins that are sticking out. Roll the dough balls in the sesame seeds and put them on a baking sheet. Working in batches, bake for 15–18 minutes until lightly browned. Cool on a wire rack for a few minutes before serving warm.

# mini pitta pizzas

It's hard to go wrong with pizza – for parties or any time.

MAKES:
8 pizzas

PREPARATION
TIME:
10 minutes

COOKING TIME:
5 minutes

STORAGE:
Not suitable
for storage.

**4 mini wholemeal pitta breads**
**40g/1½oz goat's cheese**
**4 tbsp tomato sauce (see page 117)**
**40g/1½oz mozzarella cheese, cubed**
**¼–½ tsp dried oregano**

**BASIL PESTO**
**2 tbsp pine nuts**
**60g/2¼oz/1 cup tightly packed basil leaves**
**1 garlic clove, chopped**
**4 tbsp grated Parmesan cheese**
**2 tbsp olive oil**
**¼ tsp salt**

**1** Preheat the grill to medium. Put the pine nuts for the pesto in a pan and heat over a medium-low heat, stirring continuously, until lightly toasted, then set aside to cool. Put the pitta breads on a baking sheet and lightly toast under the grill until they puff up and are lightly browned. Carefully cut them in half by slicing around the edge of each pitta with a sharp knife to produce 2 circles from each pitta.

**2** To make the pesto, put the pine nuts, basil, garlic, Parmesan, olive oil and salt in a food processor and process for 1–2 minutes until the mixture forms a thick paste. Spread 1 teaspoon of the pesto over 4 of the pitta circles, then crumble the goat's cheese over the pesto. Spread 1 tablespoon of the tomato sauce over each of the remaining 4 pitta circles and divide the mozzarella over the sauce. Put the pittas on the baking sheet, sprinkle sparingly with the oregano and grill for 2 minutes until crunchy and the cheese has melted. Serve hot.

# cherry tomatoes with hummus & capers

Most kids love tomatoes, especially sweet cherry tomatoes. These pretty bite-sized morsels can be popped into little mouths one at a time.

MAKES:
About 30

PREPARATION
TIME:
20 minutes,
plus making
the hummus

STORAGE:
Not suitable
for storage.

**30 cherry tomatoes, about 270g/9½oz**
**1 recipe quantity hummus (see page 97)**
**2 tbsp small capers or 30 large caper berries**

**1** Cut off the tops of the tomatoes and, using a melon baller or small spoon, scoop the centre and seeds out of the tomatoes and discard.

**2** Fill the tomatoes with the hummus, using a tiny spoon. Top each tomato with 4–5 tiny capers or 1 caper berry, then serve.

# ▼ sweet potato & carrot patties

These delicious patties are always a hit at parties. You'll want to make them ahead of time and keep them warm in the oven.

MAKES:
12 patties

PREPARATION TIME:
15 minutes

COOKING TIME:
30 minutes

STORAGE:
Refrigerate the cooked patties for up to 3 days.

450g/1lb sweet potatoes, cut into cubes
225g/8oz carrots, cut into thin rounds
1 tbsp sesame seeds
3–4 spring onions, trimmed and sliced into circles
wholemeal spelt flour, for coating (optional)
4 tbsp Greek yogurt
½ tsp curry powder
sliced cucumber, to serve

**1** Put the sweet potatoes and carrots in a steamer and steam, covered, over boiling water for 20 minutes or until soft. Meanwhile, put the sesame seeds in a medium saucepan and heat over a medium-low heat for 3–4 minutes, shaking the pan occasionally, until the seeds begin to brown and just start popping. Set aside.

**2** Preheat the grill to medium. Put the sweet potatoes and carrots in a bowl and mash with a fork, then mix in the sesame seeds and spring onions. Shape the mixture into 12 balls of equal size, then flatten into 6cm/2½in patties about 2cm/¾in high. If they are very sticky, sprinkle both sides with flour and put on a baking sheet. Grill for 5 minutes on each side until warmed through and lightly browned.

**3** Meanwhile, put the yogurt and curry powder in a small bowl and mix well. Serve the patties warm with the sauce and sliced cucumbers.

# cheesy polenta bites

MAKES:
80 bites

PREPARATION
TIME:
10 minutes

COOKING TIME:
20 minutes

STORAGE:
Refrigerate for
up to 3 days.

Nicholas always goes back for more and more of this simply irresistible finger food. Corn makes a nice addition at a party, and kids love the delicious melted cheese.

**butter, for greasing**
**1½ tsp salt**
**175g/6oz/1 cup polenta**
**85g/3oz Parmesan cheese,**
**  coarsely grated**
**30g/1oz Parmesan cheese,**
**  finely grated**

**1** Preheat the grill to medium and grease the bottom of a 26cm/10½in square baking tin with butter. In a heavy-based saucepan, bring 875ml/30fl oz/3½ cups water to the boil over a high heat. Add the salt and then the polenta, whisking vigorously to avoid lumps before it begins to thicken. Reduce the heat to medium-low and cook for 15 minutes, stirring continuously with a wooden spoon, until thick and stiff. Remove from the heat, then mix in the coarsely grated Parmesan cheese.

**2** Pour the polenta into the tin. Smooth out the surface using a rubber spatula. Spread from the centre outwards, pushing the polenta into the corners. Sprinkle over the finely grated Parmesan.

**3** Grill for 5 minutes until lightly browned. Leave to cool for 10 minutes until set. Cut into 2.5cm/1in squares and serve hot, warm or cold.

# tofu squares

MAKES:
24 squares

PREPARATION
TIME:
10 minutes, plus
at least 1 hour
marinating

COOKING TIME:
10 minutes

STORAGE:
Refrigerate for
up to 3 days.

Herbivores and carnivores alike will love these highly flavoured, bite-sized squares of tofu. Tofu absorbs the flavours it's cooked with, and the tamari and garlic here really add pizzazz.

**4 tbsp tamari**
**2 garlic cloves, finely**
**  chopped**
**375g/13oz firm tofu,**
**  cut into 24 cubes**
**  of equal size**
**2 tsp toasted sesame oil**

**1** Put the tamari and garlic in a large, shallow dish. Add the tofu and then turn each piece over to coat in the marinade. Cover and chill for 1 hour or overnight.

**2** Heat the sesame oil in a large frying pan over a medium-high heat. When it is hot, add the tofu and marinade. Cook for 5 minutes on each side, carefully turning the tofu squares over one by one until they are browned, the liquid has evaporated and the garlic is lightly fried. Serve hot or warm.

# cream cheese & salmon blinis

MAKES:
50 blinis

PREPARATION
TIME:
15 minutes

COOKING TIME:
20 minutes

STORAGE:
The cooled blinis
can be stored in an
airtight container
separated by
layers of baking
parchment. They
will keep in the
fridge for up to
3 days.

If everything is prepared in advance, these are easy to assemble on the day of your party but, if need be, ask someone to help you.

40g/1½oz/¼ cup
  buckwheat flour
30g/1oz/¼ cup
  wholemeal spelt flour
½ tsp baking powder
⅛ tsp salt
1 egg
5 tbsp milk
55g/2oz/¼ cup cream
  cheese
100g/3½oz smoked
  salmon, cut into
  2.5cm/1in squares

**1** Put the buckwheat flour, spelt flour, baking powder and salt in a medium bowl and mix well. Add the egg and milk and whisk for a 1–2 minutes until blended.

**2** Heat a griddle over a medium-low heat. When it is hot, drop teaspoonfuls of the batter onto the griddle, spacing them well apart as they will spread into 6cm/2½in-wide circles. If the mixture is too thick, add a little more milk. Cook for 2–3 minutes until bubbles have popped on the surface and the underside of the blinis are lightly brown. Turn them over and cook for a further 2–3 minutes until lightly browned. Remove from the griddle and leave to cool.

**3** Spread a little of the cream cheese on the top of each blini, top with 1 piece of the salmon and serve.

# sweet potato fish balls

MAKES:
36 balls

PREPARATION
TIME:
15 minutes

COOKING TIME:
25 minutes

STORAGE:
Refrigerate for
up to 2 days.

These unbelievably good fish balls are so quick to make, and they're a great addition to any party-food menu.

250g/9oz sweet potatoes,
  unpeeled, cut into
  1cm/½in cubes
225g/8oz skinned pollock
  or haddock fillet,
  roughly chopped
  (check for bones)
1 egg, beaten
¼ tsp salt

**1** Put the sweet potatoes in a steamer and steam, covered, over boiling water for 10 minutes until beginning to soften. Add the fish and continue steaming for a further 5 minutes until the fish is just cooked and the sweet potato is soft.

**2** Preheat the grill to medium-high. Transfer the sweet potato and fish to a bowl and roughly mash with a fork until the mixture comes together but is still chunky. Mix in the egg and salt. The mixture will be a little sticky. Using a large melon baller or two teaspoons, scoop portions of the mixture onto a baking sheet. Grill for 4–5 minutes on each side until lightly browned and warmed through. Serve warm.

# spelt cake

**SERVES:**
12–25

**PREPARATION TIME:**
35 minutes

**COOKING TIME:**
50 minutes

**STORAGE:**
Freeze the baked, undecorated cake for up to 1 month or refrigerate for up to 3 days.

This, for me, is the perfect party cake. Decorate it with fruit for the healthiest version or use buttercream icing for something more decadent.

170g/6oz butter, plus extra for greasing
120g/4¼oz/1 cup white spelt flour, plus flour for dusting
240ml/8fl oz/scant 1 cup rice milk
½ tsp salt
180g/6¼oz/1½ cups wholemeal spelt flour
1½ tsp baking powder
5 eggs, at room temperature
440g/15½oz/2 cups granulated sugar
1½ tsp vanilla extract
50–55 red grapes, cut in half or 60–65 blueberries (optional)

**BUTTERCREAM ICING (optional)**
450g/1lb/3⅔ cups icing sugar
185g/6½oz butter, softened
3 tbsp milk
1 tsp vanilla extract
food colouring (optional)

*fruit toppings* are delicious, healthy alternatives to sugary icings. Vitamin-packed grapes and berries can be a great solution to your child's sugar cravings.

**1** Preheat the oven to 180°C/350°F/Gas 4 and grease a 25 x 30cm/10 x 12in cake tin with butter. Line the base with baking parchment, then grease and flour it. Heat the butter, rice milk and salt in a small saucepan over a low heat until the butter has melted and the liquid is hot but not simmering (remove from the heat if necessary).

**2** In a medium bowl, sift together the flours and baking powder. In a large bowl, beat the eggs and sugar, using a whisk or an electric mixer on medium speed, for 5 minutes or until light in colour. Mix in the vanilla extract, then lower the mixer speed to low and beat the flour mixture into the eggs until just blended. Slowly add the hot rice milk mixture and beat on low speed just until smooth, pausing once to scrape down the sides of the bowl with a rubber spatula. Pour the warm batter into the cake tin.

**3** Bake for 40–45 minutes until the cake is beginning to pull away from the sides of the tin and a cocktail stick or skewer inserted in the centre comes out clean. Leave the cake to cool on a wire rack for 20 minutes, then slide a knife around the sides of the tin and turn the cake out onto the rack to cool completely.

**4** Meanwhile, make the icing, if using. Put all of the ingredients in a mixing bowl and mix on medium-high speed for 10–15 minutes until well creamed, light and fluffy, scraping down the sides of the bowl once with a rubber spatula. Stir in the food colouring, if using.

**5** If desired, cut the cake into a heart by cutting a heart shape the size of the cake out of a piece of paper. Put the cake, bottom-side up, on a large plate and cover with the paper heart. Trace around the heart with a sharp knife, then remove the paper. Holding the knife completely vertically, cut through the tracing lines to make a heart. Set aside the trimmings to snack on later.

**6** Spread or pipe the icing, if using, over the top and sides of the cake. Put the grapes, if using, around the edge. For birthdays, use the remaining grapes to form the number of your child's age in the middle of the cake; otherwise, arrange the remaining grapes on top of the cake. Serve that day.

# index